AAT L3
Final Accounts Preparation
Study Text and Exam Practice Kit

Chapter	Contents	Page
1	Types of Organisation	5
2	Accounting and Ethical Principles	19
3	Incomplete Records	35
4	Margin and Mark-Up	73
5	Preparing Accounts for Sole Traders	93
6	Preparing Accounts for Partnerships	121
7	Accounting for Partnership Goodwill	143
8	Preparing Accounts for a Limited Company	155
	Solutions to Chapter Activities	167

Introduction

This Advanced level unit is about preparing final accounts for sole traders and partnerships, and helping students to become aware of alternative business organisation structures.

This purpose of this unit is to provide the background knowledge and skills that a student needs in order to be capable of drafting accounts for sole traders and partnerships, and it provides the background knowledge of the regulations governing company accounts. A successful student will be able to complete tasks while being aware of potential ethical issues and know how to report information effectively. The student should become an accomplished member of the accounting team who is able to work with little supervision and who can see a financial picture of the organisation as a whole.

Students will be able to recognise the different types of organisations that need to prepare financial statements and will understand why such statements are important to users in the business environment. The financial accounting techniques and knowledge that they have already acquired will be developed to prepare accounting records when the records are incomplete, and students will become familiar with mark-up and margin.

Students will recognise special accounting requirements for partnerships. They will become aware of legislation and regulations governing financial statements, and will be able to recall and apply ethical knowledge to situations arising during the preparation of accounts. This unit also introduces students to the terminology and formats used by accountants in the financial statements of companies, working with the International Financial Reporting Standards (IFRS) terminology that is utilised across AAT.

Using all of this, the student will be able to prepare final accounts for sole traders and partnerships from an initial trial balance and present these to their line manager. They will then gain awareness of the more detailed requirements for the preparation of company financial statements.

Final Accounts Preparation is a mandatory unit in this qualification. It is closely linked to the Advanced level financial accounting unit, Advanced Bookkeeping, as well as to the Foundation level units, Bookkeeping Transactions and Bookkeeping Controls. In addition, it draws on the ethical principles from the Advanced level unit, Ethics for Accountants. On completion of this unit, students are prepared to start the Professional level unit, Financial Statements of Limited Companies.

Source: AAT Syllabus

Syllabus areas referenced to the study chapters (AQ2016 syllabus)

Learning outcomes	Study chapters
Distinguish between the financial recording and reporting requirements of different types of organisation	Chapter 1
Explain the need for final accounts and the accounting and ethical principles underlying their preparation	Chapter 2
Prepare accounting records from incomplete information	Chapter 3 and 4
Produce accounts for sole traders	Chapter 5
Produce accounts for partnerships	Chapter 6 and 7
Recognise the key differences between preparing accounts for a limited company and a sole trader	Chapter 8

This Study Text and Exam Practice Kit is produced by our expert team of AAT tutors. Our team have extensive experience teaching AAT and writing high quality study materials that enable you to focus and pass your exam. It covers all aspects of the syllabus in a user friendly way and builds on your understanding of each chapter by using real style exam activities for you to practice.

We also sell FIVE AAT 'real style' exam practice assessments for this subject to give lots more exam practice and the very best chance of exam success.

Visit www.acornlive.com/aat-home-study/ for more information.

Our team work very long hours to produce study material that is first class and absolutely focused on passing your exam. We hope very much that you enjoy our product and wish you the very best for exam success!

For feedback please contact our team aatlivelearning@gmail.com or safina@acornlive.com

Polite Notice! © Distributing our digital materials such as uploading and sharing them on social media or e-mailing them to your friends is copyright infringement.

Types of organisation

1.1 Introduction

This chapter will explain different organisations that need to prepare final accounts and recognise the regulations applying to each type of organisation.

Types of organisation that may be examined include:

- Sole trader
- Partnership
- Limited Liability Partnership (LLP)
- Limited Company
- Charity

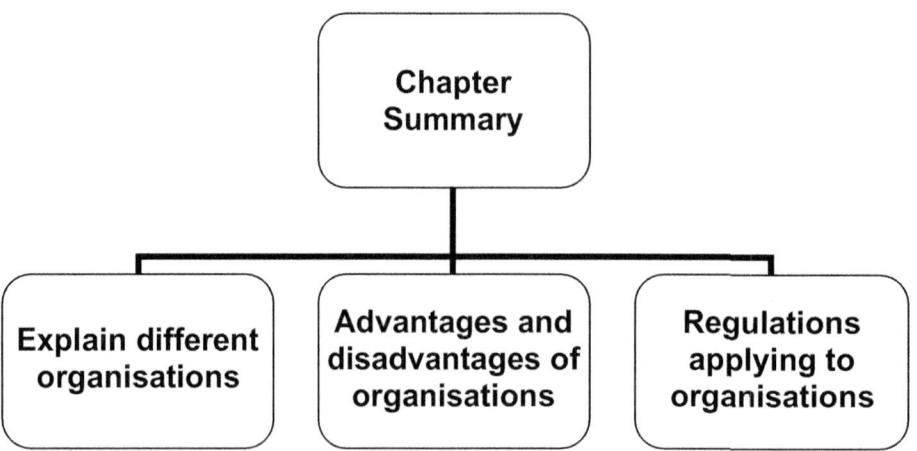

1.2 Sole traders

A sole trader is a self-employed person that runs a business. They trade on their own and are fully responsible for making their own business decisions. They are the sole proprietor (owner) of their own business and personally liable for the debts of the business.

Characteristics of a sole trader

- One single person who owns and manages a business for profit motive.
- The owner may employ staff to work for their business.
- The representation of net assets (total assets - total liabilities) in the statement of financial position is called 'capital' of the owner, which represents what the owner has invested in the business.

Advantages

- The owner has full control over the business and makes all the decisions.
- All profits earned by the business belong solely to the owner.
- Easy business to form legally and no complex accounting regulations.

Disadvantages

- The owner has 'unlimited liability' for their business debts.
- Finance is normally limited for a sole trader to fund their business.
- The owner works long hours and can't take time off for holidays or sickness.
- The owner has limited skills and expertise to do everything for their business.

Regulations applying to sole traders

A sole trader is a person that has no separate legal existence from their own business. The person and the business are treated legally as the same person, if the business cannot pay its debts, then unlimited liability exists for the sole trader. This means that if the business cannot pay its debts, the sole trader is legally obligated to pay any unpaid liabilities of the business using their own personal assets, they can be made personally bankrupt if unable to do so.

Final accounts for a sole trader are not governed by laws and accounting regulations to the same extent as limited companies (see later). There is no definitive presentation for final accounts, or any specific accounting legislation that governs how sole trader final accounts should be prepared. In most cases, just a profit or loss account is prepared as the basic information for tax return purposes.

- No accounting laws or regulations for preparing final accounts.
- Sole traders pay income tax and national insurance on profits earned by the business.
- Sole traders are responsible for submitting their own annual income tax returns and VAT returns (if the business is registered for VAT) to Her Majesty's Revenue and Customs (HMRC).

1.3 Partnerships

A partnership is when two or more self-employed persons run a business together.

Characteristics of a partnership

- Two or more persons own and manage a business for profit motive.
- The partners (owners) may employ staff to work for their business.
- The representation of net assets (total assets - total liabilities) in the statement of financial position is called 'capital', each partner (owner) would have their own capital account to represent what they have personally invested in the business.

Advantages

- Partners can provide more investment to fund the business.
- Partners can provide more skills and expertise to make the business more successful.
- Partners can give more cover to each other for sickness and holidays.
- Partners can share the risk and workload needed to run the business.
- Easy business to form legally and no complex accounting regulations.

Disadvantages

- Partners have the personal risk of poor actions or decisions by other partners.
- Partners have 'unlimited liability' for the business debts.
- Partners have equal authority to manage and control the business, this can make decisions take longer, create conflicts and disagreements.
- All profits earned by the business must be shared between partners.
- The risk of retirement, sickness or death of a partner.

Regulations applying to a partnership

- There is a statutory maximum of 20 partners allowed in a partnership, but there are many permitted exceptions such as for solicitors and accountants.
- No accounting laws or regulations for preparing final accounts.
- Partners pay income tax and national insurance on their share of profits earned from the partnership business.
- Partners are responsible for submitting their own annual income tax returns and VAT returns (if the business is registered for VAT) to Her Majesty's Revenue and Customs (HMRC).

Like a sole trader, a partner is a person that has no separate legal existence from the business, the partners and the business are treated legally as the same. If the partnership business cannot pay its debts, then unlimited liability exists for each partner. This means that if the business cannot pay its debts, each partner is legally obligated to pay any unpaid liabilities of the business using their own personal assets, each partner can be made personally bankrupt if unable to do so. It is advisable to have a partnership agreement that sets out the rights, duties and obligations of each partner.

Final accounts for a partnership are not governed by laws and accounting regulations to the same extent as limited companies (see later). There is no definitive presentation for final accounts, or any specific accounting legislation that governs how partnership final accounts should be prepared. Final accounts could be as simple as just a profit or loss account as information for each partners tax return.

1.4 Limited company

A company is a business that is run by a board of directors and owned by its shareholders. A company is a separate legal person that can enter into contracts, be sued or made bankrupt just like a real person.

Characteristics of a company

- A board of directors is appointed by the company shareholders to manage and control the company.
- Shareholders own shares (equity) in the company, which represents the ownership and voting rights of each shareholder.
- The company is a separate legal entity from its shareholders (owners).
- The company pays corporation tax on its profits earned.
- The company distributes profits earned by paying dividends to its shareholders.
- The representation of net assets (total assets - total liabilities) in the statement of financial position is called equity, which represents the capital invested by shareholders of the company.
- The company may employ staff to work for the business.

Types of company

- A private limited company uses the standard abbreviation of 'Ltd' which stands for 'limited'. This type of company is private and cannot offer it shares for sale to the general public, shares can only be sold to existing shareholders and to private investors.
- A public limited company uses the standard abbreviation of 'Plc' which stands for 'public limited company'. This type of company offers its shares for sale to the general public. Its share price is publicly quoted on a registered exchange market such as the London stock exchange, where anyone can buy or sell the shares.

Advantages

- The legal status of being a 'company' often gives more credibility to the business.
- Shareholders have 'limited liability' for debts that cannot be paid by the company.
- A public limited company has access to high levels of investment from potentially unlimited numbers of shareholders.

Disadvantages

- Complex financial reporting requirements and legal company regulations.
- Complex to form a company as a business and allot of administration, such as annual final accounts, annual returns and corporation tax returns.
- Financial information about the company is in the public domain, because final accounts need to be submitted annually to Companies House.

There can be divorce (separation) between 'ownership' and 'control' of a company, although this is more common in public limited companies, where the business can be much larger in size. This means that the directors control the assets of the company and make the day to day decisions, whereas shareholders own the company but do not participate in the running the company. This makes investing in shares risky to a shareholder because there is little transparency about what the directors are doing on a day to day basis.

The Limited Liability Act 1855 was an act of parliament in the UK that first allowed 'limited liability' for shareholders of a company. Limited liability means a shareholder (owner) can only lose what they have invested to buy their shares in the company, their personal assets are not at risk if the company fails.

Regulations applying to companies

The Companies Act is the primary source of company law that governs companies in the UK. For example, it regulates the incorporation (formation) of a company and directors' duties and responsibilities.

Accounting standards also regulate and govern extensively how company financial statements are prepared and presented. As a legal requirement the company must file annual financial statements to Companies House.

Example of company financial statements

- Statement of profit or loss.
- Statement of financial position.
- Statement of cash flows.
- Supporting notes to the financial statements.
- Directors' report to the shareholders.
- Auditor's report (smaller companies may be exempt).

A company is a separate legal person and must pay corporation tax on its profits earned, it must file an annual company tax return to HMRC.

1.5 Limited Liability Partnership (LLP)

A Limited Liability Partnership (LLP) has the characteristics of both a partnership and a company. Partners (owners) are called 'members' and the LLP give members 'limited liability' protection just like shareholders of a company. Members can only lose their capital invested in the LLP, their personal assets are not at risk if the LLP fails.

Characteristics of an LLP

- LLPs do not have shareholders or directors, they have members (owners). LLPs must have a minimum of two members, but the number of members is unlimited.
- LLPs do not file a company tax return or pay corporation tax. Members are taxed just like partners in a partnership and treated as being self-employed. Members pay income tax and national insurance on their share of profits earned from the LLP.
- The representation of net assets (total assets - total liabilities) in the statement of financial position is called 'capital', each member (owner) would have their own capital account to represent what they have personally invested in the business.
- The LLP may employ staff to work for the business.

LLPs have similar advantages and disadvantages to a partnership. An additional advantage of an LLP is 'limited liability' for its members, an additional disadvantage is the complex legal and accounting regulations that govern LLPs.

Regulations applying to LLPs

In the UK, LLPs are governed by the Limited Liability Partnership Act 2000 which came into force on 6 April 2001. Each member is not responsible or liable for another members misconduct or negligence and each member has limited liability.

An LLP is formed through the process of legal incorporation, like a company. Accounting standards also regulate and govern extensively how LLP financial statements are prepared and presented. As a legal requirement an LLP must file annual financial statements to Companies House. All members are responsible for ensuring compliance to legal and accounting regulations.

Example of LLP financial statements

- Statement of profit or loss.
- Statement of financial position.
- Statement of cash flows.
- Supporting notes to the financial statements.
- Directors' report to the shareholders.
- Auditor's report (smaller LLPs may be exempt).

1.6 Charity

Charities are non-profit making organisations (NPOs) that exist for public benefit.

Characteristics

- Non-profit making.
- Run by a Board of Trustees.
- Funded ultimately from donations made from the general public.
- Purpose must be for 'public benefit' for example, social, charitable, educational, religious or scientific aims.
- Tax exempt (charities do not pay tax).
- Staff maybe employed to work for the charity.

Regulations applying to charities

Charities are legally regulated and must follow charity laws. They are governed by a trust deed that sets out the appointment of trustees, the requirement for meetings and the preparation of annual financial statements.

Charities must be registered with the charity commission which registers and regulates charities in England and Wales. The charity commission produces guidance for trustees for how they should meet their legal duties and responsibilities.

Statements of Recommended Practice (SORPs) provide the guidance and recommendations to prepare charity accounts in accordance with UK accounting standards. Annual returns and annual financial statements must be submitted to the charity commission

Example of charity financial statements

- Statement of income and expenditure.
- Statement of financial position.
- Statement of cash flows.
- Supporting notes to the financial statements.
- Trustees annual report.
- Auditor's report (smaller charities may be exempt).

The representation of net assets (assets - liabilities) in the statement of financial position for a charity is called the 'funds' of the charity. Charities are non-profit making and if income exceeds expenditure it is called a 'surplus' (not profit) and if expenditure exceeds income it is called a 'deficit' (not a loss). Charities are tax exempt and do not pay tax on surplus they earn.

Summary of organisations

	Ownership	Management	Liability for debts	Net assets	Taxation	Distributing profits	Accounting regulations
Sole trader	Sole trader	Sole trader	Unlimited Liability for a sole trader	Capital	Individual pays income tax on profits earned	Sole trader takes drawings from the business	None
Partnership	Partners	Partners	Unlimited Liability for a partner	Capital	Individuals pay income tax on their share of profits earned	Each partner takes drawings from the business	None
Company	Shareholders	Board of Directors	Limited Liability for Shareholders	Equity	Company pays corporation tax on company profits earned	Dividends paid to shareholders from profits earned by the company	Companies Act and Accounting Standards
LLP	Members	Members	Limited Liability for Members	Capital	Individuals pay income tax on their share of profits earned	Each partner takes drawings from the business	Partnership Act, Companies Act and Accounting Standards
Charity	Public benefit	Board of Trustees	Limited Liability for Trustees	Funds	Tax Exempt	Not for profit, earns a surplus or incurs a deficit	Charity legislation and statements of recommended practice

Chapter activities

Activity 1.1

Use drag and drop to match who the senior management would be for a charity and a limited liability partnership (LLP).

| Board of Trustees |
| Board of Directors |
| Members |
| Partners |

| Charity | LLP |

Activity 1.2

Show whether the following statements are true or false.

	TRUE	FALSE
The net assets of a charity are represented as the surplus of the charity in the statement of financial position.	☐	☐
A limited liability partnership gives unlimited liability for its members.	☐	☐
Partners can provide more investment, skills and expertise to make a partnership business more successful.	☐	☐

Activity 1.3

Use drag and drop to match each advantage described to a type of organisation.

Advantage	Type of organisation
Tax exempt and does not pay tax on any surplus earned.	
Full control and makes all the key business decisions.	
Gives limited liability to its members.	

- LLP
- Charity
- Partnership
- Sole trader
- Company

Activity 1.4

Show whether the following statements are true or false.

	TRUE	FALSE
The presentation of final accounts for a sole trader is governed by complex laws and accounting regulations.	☐	☐
There generally exists a statutory maximum of 20 partners allowed in a partnership.	☐	☐
A company is a separate legal person from the shareholders (owners) of the company.	☐	☐

Activity 1.5

Show whether the following statements are true or false.

	TRUE	FALSE
Profits earned from a partnership are distributed by each partner taking drawings from the business.	☐	☐
The net assets in the statement of financial position for a company can be represented as equity.	☐	☐
Charities are not regulated to the same extent as a company.	☐	☐

End of Task

Accounting and Ethical Principles

2.1 Introduction

This chapter will focus on the primary users of final accounts and the underlying ethical and accounting principles that guide the preparation of final accounts.

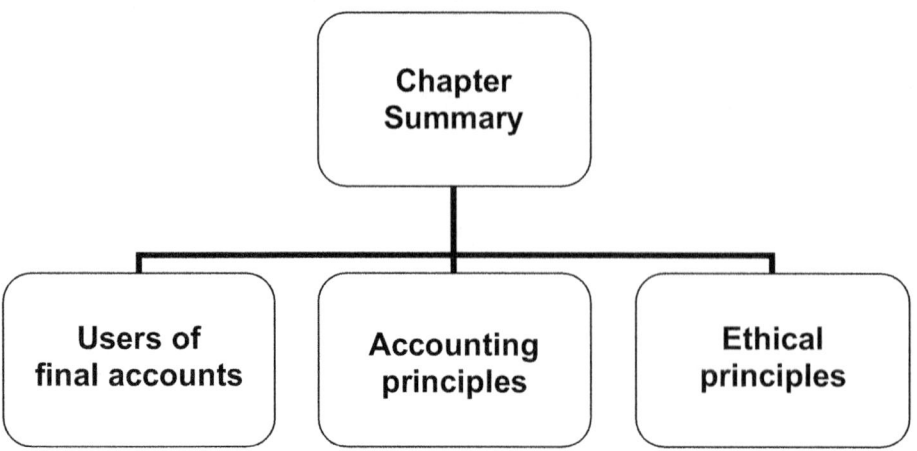

2.2 The primary users of final accounts

This section will explain the primary users of final accounts and the reasons why final accounts are needed by different users. The general purpose of final accounts is to provide information about the results of an organisations profitability, financial position and cash flows.

Final accounts

- The statement of profit or loss informs users about the ability of the business to generate profits. It also shows information about sales and the nature of expenses incurred.
- The statement of financial position informs users about the current status of the business which include net assets, liquidity, funding and its debt position.
- The statement of cash flows shows the nature of cash receipts and cash payments from operations, investing and financing activities.

The primary users of final accounts are the present and potential investors and lenders to the business. Final accounts are used by these readers (users) to make economic decisions, such as a shareholder deciding whether to buy or sell their shares, or a bank using final accounts as lending criteria to assess an application for a business loan.

Users need information from final accounts to assess the business prospects for the future and to assess the stewardship of how efficiently and effectively directors, management or owners, have used existing resources to generate cash and profits.

Investors, lenders, trade suppliers (creditors), tax authorities, employees, managers, directors, customers and the general public, may all be users of final accounts and may have different reasons for reading them.

Users of final accounts and their reasons

Users	Reasons why final accounts are needed
Owner	To assess how much profit has been generated by the business and the value of its net assets. To assess whether the business will be able to pay dividends (or drawings) in the future. To assess the risk and return from their investment and whether they should continue to invest.
Bank	To assess current debt levels of the business and its ability to meet future loan repayments and interest.
Supplier	To assess any risk of supplying goods or services on credit to the business and whether the supplier will get paid.
Management	To assess how well the business is being managed in terms of utilising assets and resources to generate cash-flows and profit.
Employee	To assess the security of their employment and the continuing profitability of the business. Interested in employment prospects, pension funding and the security of their retirement benefits.
Customer	To assess any going concern problems of the business and its ability to continue to supply goods or services in the future.
Government	HMRC, Companies House and the Office for National Statistics are examples of government agents that are interested in accounting information. HMRC needs to know the amount of tax that should be paid by the business.
General public	Individuals and groups in society may have varied interests in the activities and performance of a business. Especially if the business is well-known in the media.

2.3 Qualitative characteristics of useful financial information

The International Accounting Standards Board (IASB) is an independent, private-sector body that provides a framework to prepare final accounts.

The IASB framework

- The objective of financial reporting.
- Qualitative characteristics of useful financial information.
- Financial statements and the reporting entity.
- The elements of financial statements.
- Recognition and derecognition.
- Measurement.
- Presentation and disclosure.

Qualitative characteristics of useful financial information

Qualitative characteristics are the attributes that make financial information useful to users of final accounts. Each characteristic can be remembered using the acronym VCRUFT.

- Verifiability.
- Comparability.
- Relevance.
- Understandability.
- Faithful representation.
- Timeliness.

The 'fundamental' qualitative characteristics of useful financial information is relevance and faithful representation. There are four 'enhancing' qualitative characteristics, which include comparability, verifiability, timeliness and understandability. Enhancing characteristics support or 'enhance' the fundamental qualitative characteristics of relevance and faithful representation.

Relevance

Financial information must be capable of influencing and making a difference to the decisions of users. Relevance means information that is both material and useful to users of the final accounts. In modern times the relevance of financial reporting has been extended beyond economic decision making and may include non-financial information about the business, such as its environmental performance (carbon emissions, recycling, energy consumption) and social performance (maximising the welfare of employees, suppliers and local community).

Faithful representation

Financial information must be complete and free from material error and omission. The final accounts need to paint an objective, transparent and honest financial picture of what really happened.

Comparability

Information about a business is more useful if it can be compared with similar information to a previous year, or to another business in the same industry. Comparability enables users to identify and understand similarities and differences in business performance.

Verifiability

Verifiability gives assurance to the user that information provided is faithfully represented. Auditing accounts using an independent and external auditor can lend more credibility for information contained in a set of final accounts.

Timeliness

Timeliness means that the information is available and capable of influencing users to make economic decisions in a timely manner.

Understandability

Presenting information clearly and concisely makes it more understandable. Financial reports are prepared for users who should have reasonable knowledge of the business and its economic activities. Some information can be complex and not easily understood, but to exclude such information can make the final accounts incomplete and potentially misleading.

2.4 Accounting concepts that govern financial statements

Accounting concepts include materiality, prudence, accruals, going concern and separate entity. They act as guidelines for accountants to deal with accounting transactions and prepare final accounts.

The materiality concept

The materiality concept is an accounting rule that dictates that any transaction that significantly has an impact on the financial statements should be recognised. Sometimes an accounting matter is too small or trivial (immaterial) to be included in the financial statements.

Financial statements should be 'materially' correct. This does not mean the final accounts do not contain errors or omissions, but if materially correct a user would not be misled by the information. Financial statements need to show a true and fair view which means they are free from material errors and omissions.

The prudence concept

The prudence concept is an accounting rule that exercises conservatism and caution when making judgements about accounting transactions under conditions of uncertainty. It states that a business must not over estimate its revenues, assets and profits, or under estimate its liabilities, losses and expenses. It is a fundamental concept of accounting that increases the trustworthiness of the financial statements to show a true and fair view of events.

A provision for doubtful debts is a good example of the prudence concept in action, expenses should be recognised as soon as possible, so if a debt is doubtful (uncertain) then the prudence concept will be conservative and 'just in case, will play it safe', so an expense is provided for doubtful debts.

The accruals (matching) concept

The accruals (matching) concept is an accounting rule that recognises income earned and expenses consumed, regardless of whether the cash was received or paid. It recognises sales income and all related expenses for the same accounting year.

The concept explains why amounts recognised in the statement of profit or loss account are different to the actual cash amounts that were received or paid. For example, when telephone services are used and not paid for in the accounting year, the cash basis of accounting would not recognise any expense, however, the accruals basis would recognise the unpaid bill as an expense, because it was consumed in the accounting year. Period end adjustments such as closing inventory, depreciation charges, accruals and prepayments are all examples of the accruals concept in action.

The going concern concept

The going concern concept means to recognise a business can continue to operate and remain in business for the foreseeable future. Going concern recognises that a business can continue operating without a significant threat of liquidation or closure and remain in business for the foreseeable future (typically in the next 12 months). When a business is no longer a going concern this information is material in nature and the event should be reported and disclosed in the financial statements, assets must also be valued at their recoverable amount, which is the amount they are expected to be sold for.

The separate (business) entity concept

The separate entity concept states that transactions of a business and its owners must be recorded separately for accounting purposes. The capital account of a sole trader or partner would record separately any private transactions, such as drawings or goods taken personally by the owner of a business. In substance the business and the owners are treated as two separate people for accounting purposes.

2.5 The principles of ethics for professional accountants

The code of ethics establishes the fundamental principles of ethics for professional accountants and can be remembered using the acronym PIPCO.

- Professional competence and due care
- Integrity
- Professional behaviour
- Confidentiality
- Objectivity

Professional competence and due care

Members have a continuing duty to maintain professional knowledge and skill at a level required to ensure that a client or employer receives competent professional service based on current developments in practice, legislation and techniques. This principle requires continuing professional development (CPD) in order to remain up to date with changes in the technical environment.

Members should act diligently and in accordance with applicable technical and professional standards when providing professional services. Diligence shows care and conscientiousness to rules, regulations and the task assigned, members should avoid at all cost being careless, casual and sloppy in their work. A member should carry out their work to the best of their ability, diligently and with due care.

A professional accountant should make their own limitations known to a client or employer when tasks or advice is required. A member should not undertake a task or provide advice if they do not possess an adequate level of competence, or if without competence then to either be supervised, instructed or have their work reviewed by someone who is competent.

Integrity

Members should be straightforward and honest (truthful) in all professional and business relationships. Transparency and fairness are also important attributes of integrity. Transparency is about being open, honest and straightforward and when something goes wrong, to not try to hide it and to be upfront about the issue. Fairness is about being impartial and treating others without favouritism or discrimination.

Professional behaviour

Members should comply with relevant laws and regulations and should avoid any action that discredits their profession. Professional behaviour is about complying with laws and regulations as a minimum requirement.

Confidentiality

Members should respect the confidentiality of information acquired as a result of their professional and business relationships and should not disclose any such information to third parties without proper and specific authority, unless there is a legal or professional right or duty to disclose.

Accountants are in a unique position of having legal or privileged rights of access to information about their clients or employers business for example, salary information, sales figures, major customers and unpublished financial statements. Confidential information acquired as a result of professional and business relationships should not be used for the personal advantage of members or other third parties.

The client or employer must be able to trust the accountant not to disclose anything about their business to anyone, as it could be detrimental to their operations. It is recommended that legal advice should be sought before a member acts to avoid the risk of being sued. As a basic rule, members should not disclose any information without consent from their employer or client, they need to be discreet and consider whom disclosure can be made to.

Objectivity

Members should not allow bias, conflicts of interest or undue influence of others to override their professional or business judgement. A member must be sceptical and to 'doubt the truth', to verify sources and the validity of information. Information must be factually sound and not subjectively presented for anyone else, or the members own personal advantage.

Breaching objectivity includes falsifying or producing misleading information and deliberately omitting information to mislead a user. Members should not be associated with any form of information which is materially false, misleading, recklessly provided, or incomplete. This includes information that becomes misleading by its own omission.

Members should also avoid gifts and hospitality (unless trivial) because these may be seen as financial inducements and a threat to the principle of objectivity.

Threats to ethical principles

Threats are relationships or circumstances that can compromise a members compliance with the fundamental principles of ethics.

Intimidation threat

The threat that a professional accountant will be deterred from acting objectively because of actual or perceived pressure. For example, undue influence over the accountant because of assertion of authority, bullying or verbal threats about dismissal or litigation.

Familiarity threat

Long or close relationships with a client or employer can make an accountant too sympathetic to their interests, or too close for accepting their requests. For example, an accountant who works for a client and both have been friends for many years, or the member has someone in their family who works as a director or employee of the client. A member could fail to be objective because of the close family connection or the long relationship they have with another person.

Examples of ethical conflicts

- An 'overbearing' manager or client trying to compromise integrity (honesty) by asking a member to ignore some aspects of a technical standard or account for information falsely.
- Divided loyalties between close colleagues/clients/employers/relatives and adhering to professional standards. For example, overlooking an accounting mistake a colleague has made because it could cost them their job.
- Accepting a task without possessing adequate expertise or experience to carry out the task assigned.

Chapter activities

Activity 2.1

Jake works for an accountancy practice. Jake has gained information about a possible takeover bid of a large client of the accountancy practice and by coincidence has a close family friend who owns shares in this client.

Which ONE of the following is the most likely action that Jake should take.

Decline to discuss this matter with the close family friend.	☐
Advise the family friend of the possible takeover.	☐
Advise the family friend to hold on to their shares but don't advise them of the reasons.	☐

Activity 2.2

Rob is a trainee accountant working in a family practice that manages its own clients. Rob has been told by his boss that a client has moved to another practice because the client has found a more competitive quote for services. A few days later Rob receives a phone call from the other practice, the client has given Rob's contact details to the other practice and the caller wants certain financial figures relating to the clients previous accounting year.

Which ONE of the following principles of ethics would most likely be in breach if Rob provides any financial figures.

Confidentiality	☐
Objectivity	☐
Integrity	☐

Activity 2.3

An AAT student is asked to prepare accounts for her close friends building business that the friend and two other partners own. The business is under pressure financially and even though the AAT student does not have the necessary experience, the friend wants her to prepare financial statements to help save money for the business.

Which ONE of the following is the most likely action the AAT student should take.

To accept the task assigned because the client is a close friend.	☐
To accept the task assigned but make it known to the friend that the student does not possess the necessary experience to carry out the task assigned.	☐
To reject the task assigned but help the friend obtain competitive quotes from a qualified accountancy practice to carry out the work.	☐

Activity 2.4

Jen is an AAT student working temporarily for an employer and is helping a team to investigate and correct accounting errors. Jen is only halfway through the work she has been assigned and has already found some large errors. The accountant in charge of the team faces a tight deadline to prepare and submit the accounts and is pressurising Jen to rush through any remaining information and finish her task by today latest. Jen does not feel this will be adequate time to complete her task.

Which ONE of the following is the most likely action that Jen should take.

Obey the managers instruction without question.	☐
Present the errors that have been spotted and request a deadline extension.	☐
Resign from her position.	☐

Activity 2.5

Billy has just completed a physical inventory count for a client. He is aware there is some obsolete and very slow-moving items in the physical inventory count. Billy has a close working relationship with the client and knows that she is under pressure to deliver good profit results for her bank. The inventory value if adjusted would materially affect the financial results.

Which ONE of the following is the most likely action that Billy should take.

Do not inform the client and keep the inventory amount the same to make the accounts look good for the client. ☐

Tell the client but keep the inventory amount the same and make the accounts look good for the client. ☐

Tell the client and advise of the adjustment required and impact on profits. ☐

Activity 2.6

Show whether the following statements are true or false.

	TRUE	FALSE
A customer may use the final accounts of a business it buys goods from, to assess the debts of the business and its ability to meet future loan repayments and interest.	☐	☐
Relevance and faithful representation are the fundamental qualitative characteristics of useful financial information.	☐	☐
The prudence concept is an accounting principle that exercises caution to avoid under estimating liabilities and expenses.	☐	☐

Activity 2.7

Use drag and drop to match each explanation to an accounting principle.

Explanation	Accounting principle
A business can continue to operate and remain in business for the foreseeable future, without significant threat of liquidation or closure.	
The transactions of a business and personal transactions of its owners, must be recorded separately for accounting purposes.	
Final accounts recognise all sales income earned and all related expenses consumed for the same accounting year.	

Materiality Accruals

Separate entity Going concern

Prudence

Activity 2.8

Use drag and drop to match each explanation given to a qualitative characteristic of useful financial information.

Explanation	Qualitative characteristic
Enables users to identify similarities and differences in business performance.	
Gives assurance to the user that the information provided is faithfully represented.	
Ensures that information provided is capable of influencing and making a difference to the decisions of users.	

Timeliness Comparability

Verifiability Relevance

Understandability

Activity 2.9

Use drag and drop to match each explanation given to a user of final accounts.

Explanation	User
To assess the ability of the business to continue to supply goods or services in the future.	
To assess how much profit has been generated by the business and the value of its net assets.	
To assess the ability of the business to meet future loan repayments and interest.	

- Bank
- Employee
- Shareholder
- Customer
- Supplier

Activity 2.10

Show whether the following statements are true or false.

	TRUE	FALSE
Investors, lenders and trade suppliers would be the primary users of final accounts.	☐	☐
The enhancing qualitative characteristics of useful financial information include comparability, verifiability and faithful representation.	☐	☐
The accruals concept is an accounting principle that dictates that if a transaction has a significant impact on the final accounts, then it should be recognised.	☐	☐

End of Task

3 Incomplete Records

3.1 Introduction

Incomplete records refer to an accounting situation, where an organisation does not maintain a double-entry bookkeeping system and does not produce a trial balance. The accountant has a reduced amount of information to prepare final accounts, which may include minimal records kept such as a cash book, or even no records kept at all.

Control accounts such as the sales and purchases ledger control accounts, are useful accounting tools for incomplete records, they can be used to estimate and calculate missing figures and help prepare final accounts. Exam tasks may require you to prepare control accounts to calculate a missing figure and will require a good grasp of double entry knowledge.

A person who steals money, goods or commits a fraud, will often neglect to record accounting transactions in order to cover their tracks. Control accounts can also help identify missing items such as money or goods that have been stolen, or the drawings a sole trader has taken from the business but did not record.

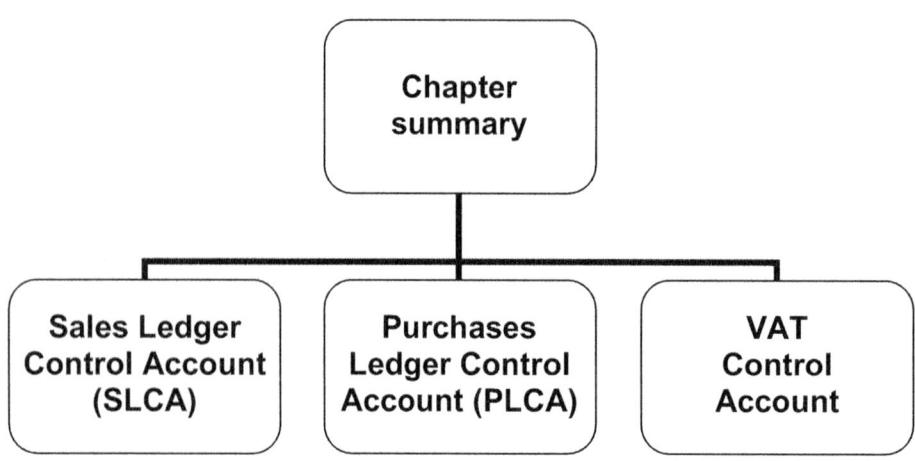

3.2 The day books (books of 'original' or 'prime entry')

Exam tasks may expect you to use the content of daybooks and distinguish between relevant and non-relevant data, to reconstruct ledger accounts such as the bank, sales, purchases and VAT ledger control accounts. You must be able to distinguish between relevant and non-relevant data from the content of daybooks provided in the exam task, not all data would be relevant, this will depend on the control account being prepared.

The day books (books of 'original' or 'prime entry')

Day books keep a record of a business's past transactions and documents such as invoices, credit notes and bank receipts and payments. At the end of each period the day books are totalled and the summary totals are then posted to the general ledger accounts using a double entry system.

Day books (the books of 'original' or 'prime entry')

- Sales Day Book (SDB records sales invoices issued, for goods sold on credit to customers).

- Sales Returns Day Book (SRDB records credit notes sent to credit customers, to reverse sales invoice amounts issued to credit customers, due to goods returned from customers or disputes with customers).

- Discounts Allowed Day Book (DADB records credit notes sent to credit customers, to reverse sales invoice amounts issued to credit customers, due to prompt payment discounts allowed for customers to settle their invoices earlier).

- Purchase Day Book (PDB records purchase invoices, for goods purchased on credit from suppliers).

- Purchase Returns Day Book (PRDB records credit notes received from credit suppliers, to reverse purchase invoice amounts issued from credit suppliers, due to goods returned back to suppliers or disputes with suppliers).

- Discounts Received Day Book (DRDB records credit notes received from credit suppliers, to reverse purchase invoice amounts issued from credit suppliers, due to prompt payment discounts allowed by suppliers to settle purchase invoices earlier).

- Cash Book (CB records all cash and bank transactions of the business).

- Petty Cash Book (PCB records very small cash transactions of the business).

- Journal Book (JN records entries made to the general ledger, for period end adjustments and the correction of errors or omissions).

Cash sales and credit sales

An important distinction exists for cash sales and credit sales. Cash sales mean the sales transaction was 'not on credit', the goods were supplied and at the same time payment was received by a customer. In this case a till (or sales) receipt is normally provided as official evidence of the sales transaction, not a sales invoice.

Cash sales do not define the payment method, payment could have been physical notes and coins, a debit card or internet payment, the term 'cash sales' just means a sale with no credit period given for a customer to pay. The double entry for cash sales (ignoring VAT) would be to debit bank and credit sales.

Credit sales, a customer would normally have a credit account with the business, they can order goods, receive delivery and are then sent a sales invoice to make payment for the goods. Credit sales (not cash sales) are recorded in a sales ledger control account (SLCA), not cash sales because cash sales are 'not on credit'. The double entry for credit sales (ignoring VAT) would be to debit SLCA and credit sales.

Cash purchases and credit purchases

The distinction between cash purchases and credit purchases is the same as for sales. A business can purchase 'goods on credit' or make 'cash purchases' from suppliers. Credit purchases (not cash purchases) are recorded in a purchases ledger control account (PLCA), not cash purchases because cash purchases are 'not on credit'. The double entry (ignoring VAT) for cash purchases would be to debit purchases and credit bank. The double entry (ignoring VAT) for credit purchases would be to debit purchases and credit PLCA.

Totalling and balancing ledger accounts

1. Look at both sides of the ledger account and find the side that has the biggest total amount (debit or credit side).
2. Add up the 'total' of all entries on the side that has the biggest total amount and place this 'total' amount on both sides of the ledger account.
3. Add up the entries on the side of the ledger account that has the smallest total amount.
4. The difference between the total amount and the entries made on the side that has the smallest total amount, is the balance carried down (c/d) at the end of the period.
5. The balance c/d is entered on the side of the ledger account that had the smallest total amount, so the totals entered on either side of the ledger account should now agree. The balance c/d calculation is an arithmetical control and considered good practice in manual ledger accounting.

The balance c/d is a balancing figure to ensure both sides of the ledger account agree at the end of the period. The true debit or true credit balance is brought down (b/d) on the opposite side, from where the balance is carried down (c/d).

3.3 The sales ledger control account (trade receivables)

A sales ledger control account (SLCA) is a general ledger account and part of a double entry system to record accounting transactions. It is a summary account that checks the arithmetical accuracy of the individual sales ledger accounts of credit customers.

Purpose of the SLCA

- Checks the accuracy of total customer balances outstanding in the sales ledger.
- Provides a quick and summarised total for customer balances outstanding in the sales ledger.
- Helps to identify any errors or missing figures.

Proforma sales ledger control accounts (SLCA) are shown below with debit and credit entries. The balance brought down (b/d) is on the debit side because a SLCA is an asset (customers who owe money to the business). All entries to a SLCA would include any VAT because the SLCA records the total amounts owed by credit customers. Credit sales (not cash sales) are recorded in a sales ledger control account (SLCA).

When preparing control accounts, exam tasks may use picklists which detail either the daybook titles (or abbreviations) or general ledger accounts for you to make your entries. Exam tasks can require the closing balance, or alternatively the closing balance can be provided in the task information and a missing figure, such as sales or discounts allowed required to be calculated.

Alternative 1 (proforma)

Sales ledger control account

	£		£
Balance b/d	X	Discounts allowed daybook (DADB)	X
Sales daybook (SDB)	X	Sales returns daybook (SRDB)	X
		Bank (CB)	X
		Set-off entries (contras)	X
		Irrecoverable debts	X
		Balance c/d	X
			X
Balance b/d	X		

Alternative 2 (proforma)

Sales ledger control account

	£		£
Balance b/d	X	Discounts allowed	X
Sales	X	Sales returns	X
		Bank	X
		PLCA (set-off entries)	X
		Irrecoverable debts	X
		Balance c/d	X
			X
Balance b/d	X		

Irrecoverable debts

An irrecoverable (bad) debt is an amount owed from a credit customer that cannot be recovered, it must be removed from the sales ledger control account and written off as an expense for the period.

Journal entry for irrecoverable debts

- Debit Irrecoverable debts (increase expenses)
- Debit VAT control account (decrease liability)
- Credit Sales ledger control account (decrease asset)

Set-off entries

A set-off (contra) entry occurs in a situation when you have a credit customer who orders goods from a business and the customer also supplies goods on credit to the business. The business would keep a customer sales ledger account for amounts 'owed to the business' and a supplier purchase ledger account for amounts 'owed from the business'.

Agreements can be made in these situations to 'set-off' balances for amounts owed between the two parties, without a cash payment. For example, the illustration provided below shows a business owes a supplier £1,200 (a liability and credit balance) and as a customer, the same supplier owes the business £2,000 (an asset and debit balance). Rather than both parties arranging a cash payment, the supplier/customer could pay £800 (£2,000 - £1,200) to the business and all credit would now be fully settled between the two parties. The double entry would be to debit Bank £800 (money received increasing the asset) and credit the SLCA £800 (decreasing this asset by the amount the customer has paid).

A balance of £1,200 still remains in both the SLCA and PLCA after all credit has been settled. A set-off entry of £1,200 is required between the two accounts (highlighted in red font) to ensure that no balance remains. The double entry for a set-off (contra) entry is always a debit entry to the PLCA and a credit entry to the SLCA.

Customer (SLCA)

Details	Amount £	Details	Amount £
Balance b/d	2,000	Bank	800
		PLCA	1,200
	2,000		2,000

Supplier (PLCA)

Details	Amount £	Details	Amount £
SLCA	1,200	Balance b/d	1,200
	1,200		1,200

Practice example

The following details are from the day books of a business for the month of April. The total balance owed from credit customers on 1 April was £17,150. Prepare a sales ledger control account using the information shown below.

Cash book - debit side

Date 20XX	Details	Bank £	Trade receivables £	Cash sales £	VAT £
1 Apr	Balance b/d	15500			
12 Apr	ABC	9800	9800		
23 Apr	OMG	9600	9600		
24 Apr	Cash sales	1200		1000	200
	Total	36100	19400	1000	200

Sales day book (SDB)

Date 20XX	Details	Invoice number	Total £	VAT £	Net £
1 Apr	OMG	00987	6600	1100	5500
2 Apr	ABC	00988	4272	712	3560
13 Apr	OMG	00989	5400	900	4500
24 Apr	XYZ	00990	1656	276	1380
26 Apr	XYZ	00991	8040	1340	6700
		Total	25968	4328	21640

Sales returns day book (SRDB)

Date 20XX	Details	CN number	Total £	VAT £	Net £
4 Apr	ABC	0012	360	60	300
29 Apr	XYZ	0014	792	132	660
		Total	1152	192	960

Discounts allowed day book (DADB)

Date 20XX	Details	CN number	Total £	VAT £	Net £
23 Apr	OMG	0013	480	80	400
		Total	480	80	400

Sales ledger control account

Details	Amount £	Details	Amount £
Total		Total	

Picklist: Balance b/d, Balance c/d, Sales day book (SDB), Cash book (CB), Sales returns day book (SRDB), Discounts allowed day book (DADB).

The solution is on the next page.

Solution to practice example

The general ledger

Sales ledger control account

Date	Details	Amount £	Date	Details	Amount £
1 Apr	Balance b/d	17150	30 Apr	CB	19400
30 Apr	SDB	25968	30 Apr	SRDB	1152
			30 Apr	DADB	480
			30 Apr	Balance c/d	22086
	Total	43118		Total	43118
1 May	Balance b/d	22086			

The dates are not normally required when preparing a control account for an exam task. An automatic sum function may also be an exam task feature, which will add up the debit and credit totals in the control account automatically.

Exam practice example

You are working on the accounting records of a sole trader for the year ended 31 March 20X8. The information provided below is to prepare a sales ledger control account. The sales figure for the year ended 31 March 20X8 is not available.

Transactions	Amount £
Balance owing from customers 1 April 20X7	7,822
Balance owing from customers 31 March 20X8	2,359
Bank receipts from credit customers	33,710
Sales returns	560
Discounts allowed	132

Using only the figures supplied, find the missing sales figure by preparing the sales ledger control account for the year ended 31 March 20X8.

Sales ledger control account

Details	Amount £	Details	Amount £
Total		Total	

Picklist: Balance b/d, Balance c/d, Bank, Sales daybook, Sales returns daybook, Discounts allowed daybook.

The solution is on the next page.

Solution to exam practice example

Sales ledger control account

Details	Amount £	Details	Amount £
Balance b/d	7,822	Bank	33,710
Sales daybook (missing figure)	28,939	Sales returns daybook	560
		Discounts allowed daybook	132
		Balance c/d	2,359
Total	36,761	**Total**	36,761

3.4 The purchase ledger control account (trade payables)

A purchases ledger control account (PLCA) is a general ledger account and part of a double entry system to record accounting transactions. It is a summary account that checks the arithmetical accuracy of the individual purchases ledger accounts of credit suppliers.

Purpose of the PLCA

- Checks the accuracy of total supplier balances outstanding in the purchases ledger.
- Provides a quick and summarised total for supplier balances outstanding in the purchases ledger.
- Helps to identify any errors or missing figures.

Proforma purchases ledger control accounts (PLCA) are shown below with debit and credit entries. The balance brought down (b/d) is on the credit side because a PLCA is a liability (the business owes money to suppliers). All entries to a PLCA would include any VAT because the PLCA records the total amounts owed to credit suppliers. Credit purchases (not cash purchases) are recorded in a purchases ledger control account (PLCA).

When preparing control accounts, exam tasks may use picklists which detail either the daybook titles (or abbreviations) or general ledger accounts for you to make your entries. Exam tasks can require the closing balance, or alternatively the closing balance can be provided in the task information and a missing figure, such as purchases or discounts received required to be calculated.

Alternative 1 (proforma)

Purchase ledger control account

	£		£
Bank (CB)	X	Balance b/d	X
Discounts received daybook (DRDB)	X	Purchases daybook (PDB)	X
Purchases returns daybook (PRDB)	X		
Set-off entries (contras)	X		
Balance c/d	X		
	X		X
		Balance b/d	X

Alternative 2 (proforma)

Purchase ledger control account

	£		£
Bank	X	Balance b/d	X
Discounts received	X	Purchases	X
Purchases returns	X		
SLCA (set-off entries)	X		
Balance c/d	X		
	X		X
		Balance b/d	X

Practice example

The following details are from the day books of a business for the month of April. The total balance owed to credit suppliers on 1 April was £7,580. Prepare a purchases ledger control account using the information shown below.

Cash book - credit side

Date 20XX	Details	Bank £	Trade payables £	Cash purchases £	VAT £	Other expenses £
12 Apr	DEF	1340	1340			
13 Apr	PQR	3600	3600			
22 Apr	Cash purchases	840		700	140	
28 Apr	Rent - SO	1500				1500
29 Apr	TUV	950	950			
30 Apr	Balance c/d	27870				
	Total	36100	5890	700	140	1500

Purchases day book (PDB)

Date 20XX	Details	Invoice number	Total £	VAT £	Net £
1 Apr	PQR	AB00987	2880	480	2400
2 Apr	DEF	0098256	672	112	560
13 Apr	DEF	0098519	480	80	400
24 Apr	TUV	1005	1068	178	890
26 Apr	PQR	AB01022	1440	240	1200
		Total	6540	1090	5450

Purchases returns day book (PRDB)

Date 20XX	Details	CN number	Total £	VAT £	Net £
4 Apr	DEF	00011	360	60	300
25 Apr	DEF	00023	792	132	660
		Total	1152	192	960

Discounts received day book (DRDB)

Date 20XX	Details	CN number	Total £	VAT £	Net £
13 Apr	PQR	AB001344	228	38	190
		Total	228	38	190

Purchases ledger control account

Details	Amount £	Details	Amount £
Total		Total	

Picklist: Balance b/d, Balance c/d, Purchases day book (PDB), Cash book (CB), Purchases returns day book (PRDB), Discounts received day book (DRDB).

The solution is on the next page.

Solution to practice example

The general ledger

Purchases ledger control account

Date	Details	Amount £	Date	Details	Amount £
30 Apr	CB	5890	1 Apr	Balance b/d	7580
30 Apr	PRDB	1152	30 Apr	PDB	6540
30 Apr	DRDB	228			
30 Apr	Balance c/d	6850			
	Total	14120		Total	14120
			1 May	Balance b/d	6850

The dates are not normally required when preparing a control account for an exam task. An automatic sum function may also be an exam task feature, which will add up the debit and credit totals in the control account automatically.

Exam practice example

You are working on the accounting records of a sole trader for the year ended 31 March 20X8. The information provided below is to prepare a purchases ledger control account. The purchases returns figure for the year ended 31 March 20X8 is not available.

Transactions	Amount £
Balance owing to suppliers 1 April 20X7	12,560
Balance owing to suppliers 31 March 20X8	8,729
Bank payments to credit suppliers	54,790
Purchases on credit	58,110
Discounts received	2,444

Using only the figures supplied, find the missing purchases returns figure by preparing the purchases ledger control account for the year ended 31 March 20X8.

Purchases ledger control account

Details	Amount £	Details	Amount £
Total		Total	

Picklist: Balance b/d, Balance c/d, Bank, Purchases, Purchases returns, Discounts received.

The solution is on the next page.

Solution to exam practice example

Purchases ledger control account

Details	Amount £	Details	Amount £
Bank	54,790	Balance b/d	12,560
Discounts received	2,444	Purchases	58,110
Purchases returns (missing figure)	4,707		
Balance c/d	8,729		
Total	70,670	**Total**	70,670

3.5 The VAT control account

The purpose of a VAT control account is to accurately record all VAT payable that has been collected from sales (outputs) and all VAT reclaimable from purchases and expenses (inputs). An accurate VAT balance can then be calculated, to be paid over to, or received from HMRC. The VAT control account provides all the necessary figures for a VAT return to be prepared by the business and submitted to HMRC.

Exam tasks may require you to prepare a VAT control account by completing the accounting entries and totalling and balancing the account. Entries will be made by selecting details from picklists available and entering the VAT figures required.

A proforma VAT control account is shown below to illustrate the debit and credit entries. The balance brought down (b/d) is shown on the credit side because VAT is normally owed to HMRC and is a liability, alternatively VAT can be an asset and the balance brought down (b/d) on the debit side, in which case VAT is owed to the business from HMRC.

VAT control account

	£		£
Purchases daybook (PDB)	X	Balance b/d	X
Cash purchases (CB)	X	Sales daybook (SDB)	X
Cash expenses (CB)	X	Cash sales (CB)	X
Sales returns daybook (SRDB)	X	Purchases returns daybook (PRDB)	X
Discounts allowed daybook (DADB)	X	Discounts received daybook (DRDB)	X
Bank (payment of VAT to HMRC)	X	Bank (refund of VAT from HMRC)	X
Balance c/d	X		
	X		X
		Balance b/d	X

When making entries to a VAT control account think about the debit and credit entries in terms of what they do, which is either increasing VAT owed (credit entry to increase liability) or decreasing VAT owed (debit entry to decrease liability).

VAT from cash sales or credit sales will increase liability to pay more VAT (credit to increase liability). Credit notes for sales returns or discounts allowed to customers, will reverse VAT owed on sales and the opposite entry (debit to decrease liability).

VAT reclaimed from cash expenses, cash purchases and credit purchases will decrease liability to pay VAT (debit to decrease liability). Credit notes for purchases returns or discounts received from suppliers, will reverse VAT reclaimed on purchases and expenses and the opposite entry (credit entry to increase liability).

A bank payment to HMRC for VAT amounts owed to HMRC, would debit the VAT control account (debit to decrease liability) and credit the bank (credit to decrease asset). A bank receipt from HMRC for VAT amounts owed from HMRC, would debit the bank (debit to increase asset) and credit the VAT control account (credit to increase liability).

The settling of credit in the SLCA (bank receipts from credit customers) or in the PLCA (bank payments to credit suppliers) do not give rise to a VAT entry in a VAT control account. Any VAT included in a bank receipt or bank payment to settle credit, has already been recorded in the sales and purchases day books. Set off (contra) entries to settle credit between the SLCA and PLCA also do not give rise to a VAT entry in a VAT control account, for the same reason.

Calculating VAT

Exam tasks may require you to identify VAT where appropriate, from a figure that includes or excludes VAT. The following examples use a sales figure to illustrate VAT workings and calculations.

Working out VAT from a net amount (excluding VAT)

A sales amount is £2,500 (net) and VAT is to be calculated on the sale.

VAT is 20% of the net amount.

Using percentages the amount is (£2,500 ÷ 100%) = £25 for every 1% x 20% = £500.

The VAT amount could also be calculated by multiplying the net sales amount by the fraction 20/100 and rounded to the lowest common denominator is 1/5 as a fraction.

1/5 x £2,500 = £500.

The fraction 1/5 (1 ÷ 5) is also 0.2 as a decimal.

0.2 x £2,500 = £500.

Working out VAT from a total gross amount (including VAT)

A sales amount is £3,000 (gross) and VAT is to be calculated on the sale.

As a percentage the amount of £3,000 represents 120% because 100% is the net amount and 20% has been added for VAT.

Using percentages the amount is (£3,000 ÷ 120%) = £25 for every 1% x 20% = £500.

The VAT amount could also be calculated by multiplying the gross sales amount by the fraction 20/120 and rounded to the lowest common denominator is 1/6 as a fraction.

1/6 x £3,000 = £500.

Practice example

The following details are from the day books of a business for the month of April. The VAT balance owing to HMRC on 1 April was £3,488. Prepare a VAT control account using the information shown below.

Cash book - credit side

Date 20XX	Details	Bank £	Trade payables £	Cash purchases £	VAT £	Other expenses £
12 Apr	DEF	1340	1340			
13 Apr	PQR	3600	3600			
22 Apr	Cash purchases	840		700	140	
28 Apr	Rent - SO	1500				1500
29 Apr	TUV	950	950			
30 Apr	Balance c/d	27870				
	Total	36100	5890	700	140	1500

Purchases day book (PDB)

Date 20XX	Details	Invoice number	Total £	VAT £	Net £
1 Apr	PQR	AB00987	2880	480	2400
2 Apr	DEF	0098256	672	112	560
13 Apr	DEF	0098519	480	80	400
24 Apr	TUV	1005	1068	178	890
26 Apr	PQR	AB01022	1440	240	1200
		Total	6540	1090	5450

Purchases returns day book (PRDB)

Date 20XX	Details	CN number	Total £	VAT £	Net £
4 Apr	DEF	00011	360	60	300
25 Apr	DEF	00023	792	132	660
		Total	1152	192	960

Discounts received day book (DRDB)

Date 20XX	Details	CN number	Total £	VAT £	Net £
13 Apr	PQR	AB001344	228	38	190
		Total	228	38	190

Cash book - debit side

Date 20XX	Details	Bank £	Trade receivables £	Cash sales £	VAT £
1 Apr	Balance b/d	15500			
12 Apr	ABC	9800	9800		
23 Apr	OMG	9600	9600		
24 Apr	Cash sales	1200		1000	200
	Total	36100	19400	1000	200

Sales day book (SDB)

Date 20XX	Details	Invoice number	Total £	VAT £	Net £
1 Apr	OMG	00987	6600	1100	5500
2 Apr	ABC	00988	4272	712	3560
13 Apr	OMG	00989	5400	900	4500
24 Apr	XYZ	00990	1656	276	1380
26 Apr	XYZ	00991	8040	1340	6700
		Total	25968	4328	21640

Sales returns day book (SRDB)

Date 20XX	Details	CN number	Total £	VAT £	Net £
4 Apr	ABC	0012	360	60	300
29 Apr	XYZ	0014	792	132	660
		Total	1152	192	960

Discounts allowed day book (DADB)

Date 20XX	Details	CN number	Total £	VAT £	Net £
23 Apr	OMG	0013	480	80	400
		Total	480	80	400

VAT control account

Date	Details	Amount £	Date	Details	Amount £
	Total			Total	

Picklist: Balance b/d, Balance c/d, Sales day book (SDB), Cash book (CB), Sales returns day book (SRDB), Discounts allowed day book (DADB), Purchases day book (PDB), Purchases returns day book (PRDB), Discounts received day book (DRDB).

The solution is on the next page.

Solution to practice example

The general ledger

VAT control account

Date	Details	Amount £	Date	Details	Amount £
30 Apr	CB (Cash purchases)	140	1 Apr	Balance b/d	3488
30 Apr	PDB	1090	30 Apr	CB (Cash sales)	200
30 Apr	DADB	80	30 Apr	SDB	4328
30 Apr	SRDB	192	30 Apr	PRDB	192
30 Apr	Balance c/d	6744	30 Apr	DRDB	38
	Total	8246		**Total**	8246
			1 May	Balance b/d	6744

The dates are not normally required when preparing a control account for an exam task. Alternative details may be used for the picklist in an exam task to make entries to a VAT control account. For example rather than PDB (see above), the picklist could use details such as 'purchase day book' or 'purchases'. An automatic sum function may also be an exam task feature, which will add up the debit and credit totals in the control account automatically.

3.6 The bank and cash accounts

Recording transactions in a bank ledger account

- A bank balance in DEBIT means a positive bank balance (money in the bank) and is an 'asset'.
- A bank balance in CREDIT means the bank account is overdrawn (money is owed to the bank) and is a 'liability'.
- To increase the bank balance, debit receipts to the bank ledger account.
- To decrease the bank balance, credit payments to the bank ledger account.

Recording transactions in a cash ledger account

A cash account may also be kept that represents physical notes and coins held in a safe, cash register or cash tin (money not deposited in the bank account). Cash in hand is an asset and unlike the bank account it cannot be overdrawn (a liability). Cash is either held as an asset, or not held at all. The double entry principle for recording receipts and payments for cash is the same as the bank.

- A cash balance would be in DEBIT and is an 'asset'.
- To increase the cash balance, debit receipts to the cash ledger account.
- To decrease the cash balance, credit payments to the cash ledger account.

Practice example

The following details relate to the business bank account of a sole trader for the month of June. The bank balance was overdrawn by £6,708 on 1 June. Prepare a bank ledger account using the information shown below.

Receipts and payments recorded in the bank account include:

Amounts paid to suppliers	29,200
Amounts received from credit customers	66,004
HMRC - VAT refund	1,026
Motor expenses	3,920
Staff wages	2,500
Loan repayment	1,200
Motor vehicles	6,810
Bank charges and interest	1,762

Bank account

Details	Amount £	Details	Amount £
Total		Total	

Picklist: Balance b/d, Balance c/d, Sales ledger control, Purchase ledger control, HMRC, Motor expenses, Staff wages, Loan repayment, Motor vehicles, Bank charges and interest.

The solution is on the next page.

Solution to practice example

Bank account

Details	Amount £	Details	Amount £
Sales ledger control	66,004	Balance b/d	6,708
HMRC	1,026	Purchase ledger control	29,200
		Motor expenses	3,920
		Staff wages	2,500
		Loan repayment	1,200
		Motor vehicles	6,810
		Bank charges and interest	1,762
		Balance c/d	14,930
Total	67,030	**Total**	67,030
Balance b/d	14,930		

The dates are not normally required when preparing a control account for an exam task. An automatic sum function may also be an exam task feature, which will add up the debit and credit totals in the control account automatically.

The bank account balance of £6,708 started overdrawn (credit balance) on 1 June, a liability owed by the business. The balance c/d of £14,930 (which would be on 30 June) is on the credit side, this amount of £14,930 would be brought down (b/d) on the debit side at the beginning of the next month (which would be on 1 July) and is an asset owned by the business.

Practice example

A retailer that sells goods to the general public keeps a cash till for recording its sales transactions. The following details relate to cash transactions for its cash till for the month of June.

- The cash till had a float (balance) of £350 on 1 June.
- The cash till had a float (balance) of £200 on 30 June.
- Sales (till receipts) for the month were £7,822.
- Cash till receipts deposited in the bank account for the month was £4,822.

The business owner is a sole trader and takes money from the cash till as drawings. Any remaining cash from the cash till is deposited in the business bank account.

Using only the figures supplied, find the missing drawings figure by preparing a cash account for the month of June.

Cash account

Details	Amount £	Details	Amount £
Total		Total	

Picklist: Balance b/d, Balance c/d, Sales, Bank, Drawings.

The solution is on the next page.

Solution to practice example

Cash account

Details	Amount £	Details	Amount £
Balance b/d	350	Bank	4,822
Sales	7,822	Drawings (missing figure)	3,150
		Balance c/d	200
Total	8,172	Total	8,172

Chapter activities

Activity 3.1

A sales ledger control account for the month of September is being prepared.

Transactions	Amount £
Balance owing 1 September	6,782
Payments received by cheque	17,822
Goods sold	24,021
Sales returns	3,410
Discounts allowed	1,244

Record these transactions in the sales ledger control account and show the balance carried down.

Picklist: Balance b/d, Balance c/d, Bank, Discounts allowed, Discounts received, Purchases, Sales, Purchases returns, Sales returns.

Sales ledger control account

Details	Amount £	Details	Amount £
Total		Total	

Activity 3.2

A purchases ledger control account for the month of September is being prepared.

Transactions	Amount £
Balance owing 1 September	7,830
Payments made by cheque	8,822
Goods purchased	14,521
Purchases returns	450
Discounts received	559

Record these transactions in the purchases ledger control account and show the balance carried down.

Picklist: Balance b/d, Balance c/d, Bank, Discounts allowed, Discounts received, Purchases, Sales, Purchases returns, Sales returns.

Purchases ledger control account

Details	Amount £	Details	Amount £
Total		Total	

Activity 3.3

The VAT control account for the month of September is being prepared. The balance brought down has already been entered at the beginning of September, the following transactions have not yet been recorded in the VAT control account.

- VAT total in the sales daybook   £3,492
- VAT total in the sales returns day book   £230
- VAT total in the purchases daybook   £1,299
- VAT total in the purchases returns day book £56
- VAT paid to HM Revenue and customs   £2,884
- VAT total in the discounts allowed day book £455
- VAT total in the discounts received day book £325

Complete the VAT control account by placing the entries on the debit or credit side:

- **enter the VAT transactions for the month**
- **show the balance carried down and whether it will be a debit or credit balance**
- **insert the total that will be shown in both the debit and credit columns after the account has been balanced**

Picklist: Balance b/d, Balance c/d, Purchases daybook, Sales daybook, Bank, Purchases returns daybook, Sales returns day book, Discounts received, Discounts allowed, Cash sales, Cash purchases.

VAT control account

Details	Amount £	Details	Amount £
		Balance b/d	2350
Total		Total	

Activity 3.4

This task is about reconstructing ledger accounts.

You are working on the accounting records of a sole trader to the year ended 30 June 20X8.

You have the following information:

Day book summaries	Goods £	VAT £	Total £
Sales	56,000	11,200	67,200
Sales returns	750	150	900
Discounts allowed	2,400	480	2,880
Purchases	32,720	6,544	39,264
Purchase returns	3,000	600	3,600
Discounts received	Not available		
Further information	Net £	VAT £	Total £
Motor expenses	1,242	248	1,490

All sales were on credit terms.
A contra entry of £500 was made between the sales ledger and purchase ledger.
Motor expenses are not processed through the purchase day book, all VAT is recoverable.
The trader took advantage of any prompt payment discounts whenever offered.
The trader made cash purchases, the total amount was paid through the bank account, but this figure is missing.

Balances as at	30 June 20X7 £	30 June 20X8 £
Trade receivables	8,500	not available
Trade payables	6,550	19,659
Closing inventory	5,000	8,900
Bank	3,402 debit	7,311 debit
VAT	5,341 credit	not available

Receipts and payments recorded in the bank account include:

Amounts to suppliers	19,655
Amounts from credit customers	45,620
Payment of VAT to HMRC	6,711
Motor expenses	1,490
Staff wages	3,025
Loan repayment	1,500
Drawings	3,500
Bank charges and interest	430

Picklist: Purchases ledger control, Sales ledger control, Balance b/d, Balance c/d, Bank, Motor expenses, Staff wages, Loan repayment, Drawings, Bank charges and interest, Inventory, Purchases, Sales, Sales returns, Purchase returns, Discounts allowed, Discounts received, VAT.

(a) Using only the figures supplied, find the closing balance for the sales ledger control account for the year ended 30 June 20X8.

Sales ledger control account

	£		£
	0		0

(b) Find the cash purchases figure including VAT by preparing the bank account for the year ended 30 June 20X8.

Bank

	£		£
	0		0

(c) Find the total discounts received figure including VAT by preparing the purchase ledger control account for the year ended 30 June 20X8.

Purchase ledger control account

	£		£
	0		0

(d) Using only the figures from the task information provided, find the closing balance on the VAT account for the year ended 30 June 20X8. Note: the business is not charged VAT on loan repayments, wages or bank charges and interest.

VAT control account

	£		£
	0		0

Activity 3.5

This task is about reconstructing ledger accounts.

You are working on the accounting records of a business for the year ended 31 January 20X5.

You have the following information:

Day book summaries	Goods £	VAT £	Total £
Sales	78,220	15,644	93,864
Sales returns	not available		
Purchases	not available		
Purchase returns	500	100	600

VAT on discounts has been correctly adjusted in the sales and purchases daybooks.

All purchases and sales for the year were on credit terms.

A contra entry of £4,000 was made between the sales ledger and purchase ledger during the year.

An irrecoverable debt of £3,600 including VAT has been written off for the year ended 31 January 20X5.

Balances as at	31 January 20X4 £	31 January 20X5 £
Trade receivables	25,760	36,722
Trade payables	9,522	18,672
Bank	14,543 debit	not available
VAT	344 credit	not available

Receipts and payments recorded in the bank account include:

Amounts to suppliers	43,200
Amounts from credit customers	66,544
HMRC - VAT refund	526
Motor expenses	1,990
Staff wages	4,000
Loan repayment	1,234
Motor vehicle	22,680
Bank charges and interest	262

(a) Find the total sales returns by preparing the sales ledger control account for the year ended 31 January 20X5.

Picklist: Sales ledger control, Purchases ledger control, Irrecoverable debts, Balance b/d, Balance c/d, Bank, Motor expenses, Motor vehicle, Loan, Purchase daybook, Wages, Sales daybook, Sales returns daybook, Purchase returns daybook, Discounts allowed day book, Discounts received daybook, Bank charges and interest, VAT.

Sales ledger control account

	£		£
	0		0

(b) Find the total purchases by preparing the purchase ledger control account for the year ended 31 January 20X5.

Purchase ledger control account

	£		£
	0		0

The totals recorded in the cash book for the year ended 31 January 20X5 were:

Receipts	£67,070
Payments	£73,366

(c) Assuming there are no year adjustments, what would be the opening bank account balance in the general ledger as at 1 February 20X5. Do NOT enter a negative figure.

Bank account balance 1 February 20X5   £ 6,296

Picklist: debit or credit   credit

End of Task

4 Margin and Mark-up

4.1 Introduction

This chapter will focus on the meaning of sales margin and mark-up and the difference between them.

Exam tasks may expect the following:

- Calculate mark-up and margin.
- Use mark-up and margin to calculate missing figures.
- Use cost of goods sold (cost of sales) to determine a missing figure.
- Adjust data for VAT from data provided.

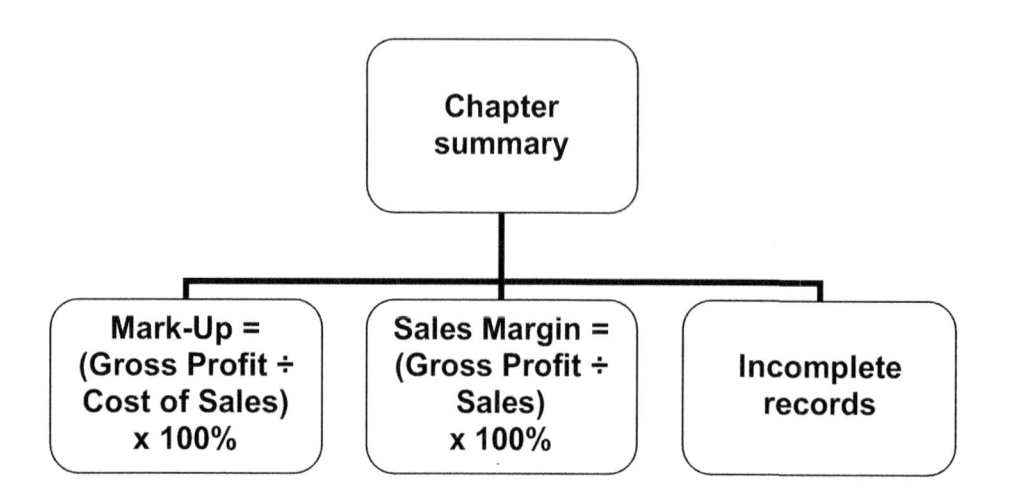

Chapter summary
- Mark-Up = (Gross Profit ÷ Cost of Sales) x 100%
- Sales Margin = (Gross Profit ÷ Sales) x 100%
- Incomplete records

4.2 The trading account

A trading account is the top section of a statement of profit or loss account. The cost of goods sold (cost of sales) is deducted from sales income, to show the amount of gross profit earned for the accounting period. It does not include other deductions for expenses, such as rent, advertising or staff wages.

Example of a trading account

	£	£
Sales		20,000
Less: Cost of sales		
Opening inventory	2,000	
Purchases	17,000	
	19,000	
Closing inventory	-3,000	
Cost of goods sold		16,000
Gross profit		4,000

Purchases represent an expense incurred for the 'cost of goods for resale' by a business, for example a grocer buys bread, milk and newspapers from suppliers and resells these goods to the general public. Sales represent the income earned from the resale of the bread, milk and newspapers purchased.

To arrive at the cost of goods sold (cost of sales) for an accounting period, opening inventory (unsold purchases at the beginning of the accounting period) is added to purchases incurred during the accounting period and closing inventory (unsold purchases at the end of the accounting period) is then deducted.

The above trading account shows that opening inventory (£2,000) is added to purchases (£17,000) and the total is £19,000 (£2,000 + £17,000). Closing inventory (£3,000) is then deducted to arrive at £16,000 (£19,000 - £3,000) cost of goods sold for the period.

Adjusting purchases for opening and closing inventory levels, removes the 'cost of goods unsold' and matches only the 'cost of goods sold' to sales income earned for the accounting period. The opening and closing inventory adjustment is because of the accruals (or matching) concept, sales income and all related expenses are being matched together in the same accounting period.

Sales income of £20,000 is matched to cost of sales of £16,000 for the same accounting period. The gross profit earned is £4,000 (£20,000 - £16,000).

Adjusting data for VAT

Sales, purchases and inventory figures in a trading account should be recorded exclusive of VAT. The exam assumption is that the business is VAT registered and therefore would post all VAT amounts to a VAT control account. Sales (income) and purchases (expenses) should be recorded exclusive of VAT. If an exam task provides a VAT inclusive figure, then VAT must be removed to determine the sales or purchases figure to include in a trading account. If no VAT is mentioned then always assume a figure is exclusive of VAT.

4.3 Sales margin and mark-up

Mark-up percentage

The mark-up percentage is a profitability measure. It represents the amount of gross profit added to the cost of goods sold (excluding VAT) to determine a selling price (excluding VAT).

Calculation of mark-up percentage

$$\frac{\text{Gross Profit}}{\text{Cost of Goods Sold}} \times 100\% = \text{Mark-up }\%$$

Using the example of the trading account shown earlier:

- Gross Profit (GP) ÷ Cost of Sales (COS) x 100% = Mark-up %.
- £4,000 ÷ £16,000 x 100% = Mark-up 25%.

Mark-up is a useful profit measure. 25% mark-up would mean the business earns 25 pence of gross profit for every £1 of cost of sales. If mark-up and a cost of sales amount is known, this information can calculate a missing gross profit and sales figure.

If mark-up is 25% and cost of sales is £16,000. A mark-up of 25% means gross profit is 25% of cost of sales, therefore cost of sales £16,000 ÷ 100% x 25% = £4,000 gross profit. If cost of sales is £16,000 and gross profit is £4,000, then sales must be £16,000 + £4,000 = £20,000.

Calculation of sales margin percentage

The sales margin percentage is a profitability measure, similar to mark-up. It represents the amount of gross profit generated from sales income earned (excluding VAT). Sales margin is useful to identify what products sold are the most and the least profitable.

$$\frac{\text{Gross Profit}}{\text{Sales}} \times 100\% = \text{Sales Margin \%}$$

Using the example of the trading account shown earlier:

- Gross Profit (GP) ÷ Sales x 100% = Sales Margin %.
- £4,000 ÷ £20,000 x 100% = Sales Margin 20%.

Sales margin is a useful profit measure. 20% sales margin would mean the business earns 20 pence of gross profit for every £1 of sales. If the sales margin and sales amount is known, this information can calculate a missing gross profit and cost of sales figure.

If sales margin is 20% and sales is £20,000. Sales margin of 20% means that gross profit is 20% of sales, therefore sales £20,000 ÷ 100% x 20% = £4,000 gross profit. If sales is £20,000 and gross profit is £4,000, then cost of sales must be £20,000 - £4,000 = £16,000.

Practice example

A sole trader has the following amounts for the year ended 31 March 20X7.

- Sales £60,000 inclusive of VAT
- Purchases £34,000 exclusive of VAT
- Opening inventory £8,000
- Closing inventory £4,500

Prepare a trading account using the information shown above. Calculate the mark-up and margin percentage (to two decimal places).

Trading account for the year ended 31 March 20X7

	£	£
Sales		
Less: Cost of sales		
Opening inventory		
Purchases		
Closing inventory		
Cost of goods sold		
Gross profit		

The solution is on the next page.

Solution to practice example

Trading account for the year ended 31 March 20X7

	£	£
Sales		50,000
Less: Cost of sales		
Opening inventory	8,000	
Purchases	34,000	
	42,000	
Closing inventory	-4,500	
Cost of goods sold		37,500
Gross profit		12,500

Sales working:

- All figures in a trading account must exclude VAT.
- Sales of £60,000 include VAT.
- £60,000 x 1/6 = £10,000 VAT included in the sales figure.
- £60,000 - £10,000 = £50,000 sales excluding VAT.

Purchases are exclusive of VAT. No VAT is mentioned about the value of opening and closing inventory, so always assume these figure are exclusive of VAT.

Calculation of mark-up

- Gross Profit (GP) ÷ Cost of Sales (COS) x 100% = Mark-up %.
- £12,500 ÷ £37,500 x 100% = Mark-up 33.33%.

A 33.33% mark-up would mean the business earns 33.33 pence of gross profit for every £1 of cost of sales.

Calculation of sales margin

- Gross Profit (GP) ÷ Sales x 100% = Sales Margin %.
- £12,500 ÷ £50,000 x 100% = Sales Margin 25%.

A 25% sales margin would mean the business earns 25 pence of gross profit for every £1 of sales.

4.4 Incomplete records

Exam tasks may expect that a missing figure is calculated using cost of goods sold, mark-up and sales margin.

A good approach to this type of exam task would be:

1. Remove any VAT amounts from sales or purchases figures (if inclusive of VAT).
2. Construct a trading account and include all figures from the exam task.
3. Use mark-up or margin to determine a gross profit figure (if missing).
4. Use how a trading account is prepared to calculate any final missing figures.

Practice example

The following details exist for a business.

- Purchases £74,000.
- Opening inventory £7,600.
- Cost of sales £66,000.

Calculate the missing figure for closing inventory.

The solution is on the next page.

Solution to practice example

	£
Opening inventory	7,600
Purchases	74,000
(£7,600 + £74,000) =	81,600
Closing inventory (missing figure)	-15,600
Cost of goods sold	66,000

Workings:

- No VAT is mentioned, so always assume figures are exclusive of VAT unless the information states otherwise.
- Construct a trading account and include all figures from the exam task. This would include opening inventory, purchases and cost of sales.
- Opening inventory and purchases added together is £81,600 (£7,600 + £74,000).
- Cost of sales is £66,000.
- Using the logic of a trading account, then the closing inventory figure must be £15,600 (£81,600 - £66,000).

Practice example

The following details exist for a business.

- Sales £120,000.
- Sales margin is 25%.
- Opening inventory £7,600.
- Closing inventory £12,600.

Calculate the missing figure for purchases.

The solution is on the next page.

Solution to practice example

	£	£
Sales		120,000
Less: Cost of sales		
Opening inventory (given)	7,600	
Purchases (£102,600 - £7,600)	95,000	
(£90,000 + £12,600)	102,600	
Closing inventory (given)	-12,600	
Cost of goods sold (£120,000 - £30,000)		90,000
Gross profit (25% x £120,000)		30,000

Workings:

- No VAT is mentioned, so always assume figures are exclusive of VAT unless the information states otherwise.
- Construct a trading account and include all figures from the exam task. This would include sales, opening inventory and closing inventory.
- Sales margin can be used to determine the gross profit figure. 25% margin means gross profit is 25% of sales. Sales £120,000 ÷ 100% x 25% = £30,000 gross profit.
- Cost of goods sold is the difference between sales £120,000 and gross profit £30,000. Cost of goods sold is £90,000 (£120,000 - £30,000).
- Using the logic of the trading account, £12,600 closing inventory is added back to the cost of goods sold of £90,000. £102,600 (£12,600 + £90,000) would be the opening inventory and purchases figures added together.
- Using the logic of the trading account, if opening inventory and purchases added together is £102,600, the missing figure for purchases must be £95,000 (£102,600 - £7,600 opening inventory).

Practice example

The following details exist for a business.

- Mark-up is 50%.
- Opening inventory £4,300.
- Closing inventory £2,200.
- Purchases £95,000.

Calculate the missing figure for sales (round all figures to the nearest whole pound).

The solution is on the next page.

Solution to practice example

	£	£
Sales (£48,550 + £97,100)		145,650
Less: Cost of sales		
Opening inventory (given)	4,300	
Purchases (given)	95,000	
	99,300	
Closing inventory (given)	-2,200	
Cost of goods sold		97,100
Gross profit (50% x £97,100)		48,550

Workings:

- No VAT is mentioned, so always assume figures are exclusive of VAT unless the information states otherwise.
- Construct a trading account and include all figures from the exam task. This would include purchases, opening inventory and closing inventory.
- The information given can calculate cost of sales which is £97,100 (£4,300 + £95,000 - £2,200).
- Mark-up can be used to determine the gross profit figure. 50% mark-up means gross profit is 50% of cost of sales. Cost of sales £97,100 ÷ 100% x 50% = gross profit of £48,550.
- Using the logic of the trading account, sales can be calculated by adding together the cost of sales (£97,100) and gross profit (£48,550). The missing figure for sales must be £145,650 (£97,100 + £48,550).

Exam tasks may not provide data separately for the value of opening and closing inventory, alternatively the data could give only the increase or decrease in value of inventory for the period. The increase or decrease means the change between the value of opening inventory and closing inventory for the period. Despite this data being more limited, it is still possible to calculate a missing figure for either purchases or the cost of goods sold.

Example

The following information is available for a business:

- Cost of sales is £37,500.
- Inventory levels decreased for the period by £3,500.

Calculate the missing figure for purchases.

Opening and closing inventory levels are unknown, the following logic can be used to solve the missing figure for purchases.

Solution

- Inventory levels decreased by £3,500.
- If inventory levels decrease, then closing inventory must be lower than opening inventory, therefore £3,500 more is charged to cost of sales, compared with purchases.
- If £3,500 is deducted from cost of sales (£37,500), this will calculate the missing figure for purchases. Purchases would be £34,000 (£37,500 - £3,500).

Another logical way of dealing with the above problem would be to construct a working for cost of sales, like the one illustrated below. Insert the cost of sales figure of £37,500 and make up any assumption about the value of opening inventory. The workings show that opening inventory of £8,000 was selected as a 'made up' figure and so to force things to work, the closing inventory figure would be £4,500 because inventory levels decreased by £3,500. Purchases can then be calculated as a balancing figure.

Opening inventory (made up)	8,000
Purchases (balancing figure)	34,000
	42,000
Closing inventory (inventory levels decrease by £3,500)	-4,500
Cost of goods sales (given)	37,500

You can select any value of opening inventory in the approach used above, but do need to ensure that closing inventory is increased or decreased by the right amount, compared to opening inventory.

Example

The following information is available for a business:

- Cost of sales is £30,500.
- Inventory levels increased for the period by £3,500.

Calculate the missing figure for purchases.

Opening and closing inventory levels are unknown, the following logic can be used to solve the missing figure for purchases.

Solution

- Inventory levels increased by £3,500.
- If inventory levels increase, then closing inventory must be higher than opening inventory, therefore £3,500 less is charged to cost of sales, compared with purchases.
- If £3,500 is added to cost of sales (£30,500), this will calculate the missing figure for purchases. Purchases would be £34,000 (£30,500 + £3,500).

Another logical way of dealing with the above problem would be to construct a working for cost of sales, like the one illustrated below. Insert the cost of sales figure of £30,500 and make up any assumption about the value of opening inventory. The workings show that opening inventory of £4,500 was selected as a 'made up' figure and so to force things to work, the closing inventory figure would be £8,000 because inventory levels increased by £3,500. Purchases can then be calculated as a balancing figure.

Opening inventory (made up)	4,500
Purchases (balancing figure)	34,000
	38,500
Closing inventory (inventory levels increase by £3,500)	-8,000
Cost of goods sales (given)	30,500

You can select any value of opening inventory in the approach used above, but do need to ensure that closing inventory is increased or decreased by the right amount, compared to opening inventory.

Chapter activities

Activity 4.1

You have the following information about a business for the year ended 31 March 20X9.

Using the information below, complete the following tasks.

- Sales for the year inclusive of VAT was £360,000.
- The business operates with a sales margin of 20%.
- Opening inventory at the start of the year was £48,000.
- Purchases for the year inclusive of VAT was £252,000.

(a) Calculate the cost of goods sold for the year ended 31 March 20X9.

£ [ ]

Use the information shown below to answer part (b).

- Due to a fire on 31 March 20X9, most of the closing inventory was destroyed.
- The value of closing inventory that remained after the fire was £1,500.

(b) Calculate the value of the closing inventory destroyed in the fire.

£ [ ]

Activity 4.2

You have the following information about a business for the year ended 30 June 20X7.

Using the information below, complete the following tasks.

- Cost of goods sold for the year ended 30 June 20X7 was £242,610.
- Inventory increased by £21,220 during the year.

Complete the following tasks:

(a) Calculate the value of purchases for the year ended 30 June 20X7.

£ [   ]

The business sells its goods at a mark-up of cost plus 40%.

(b) Calculate the missing sales figure to go in the trial balance as at 30 June 20X7.

£ [   ]

Activity 4.3

- A business sold goods to a customer for £1,500 including VAT.
- Standard rated VAT of 20% applies to all sales and purchases made.
- The sales margin for the goods sold is 25%.

Calculate the original cost of the goods sold to the customer excluding VAT. Round your answer to the nearest 2 decimal places.

£ [   ]

Activity 4.4

You have the following information about a business for the year ended 31 January 20X2.

- Purchases for the year ended 31 January 20X2 was £180,500.
- Inventory decreased by £21,500 during the year.
- Mark-up is 35%.

Calculate sales for the year ended 31 January 20X2. Round your answer to the nearest whole pound.

£ ☐

End of Task

5 Preparing Accounts for Sole Traders

5.1 Introduction

This chapter will focus on how to prepare a statement of profit or loss and statement of financial position for a sole trader. The layout for the statement profit or loss and statement of financial position will be provided in the exam task for you to complete.

This chapter also focuses on how to prepare a capital account for a sole trader. Exam tasks may expect you to calculate the opening, or closing balance for a capital account and to record entries for a capital account, such as for drawings, capital injections and profits earned by the business.

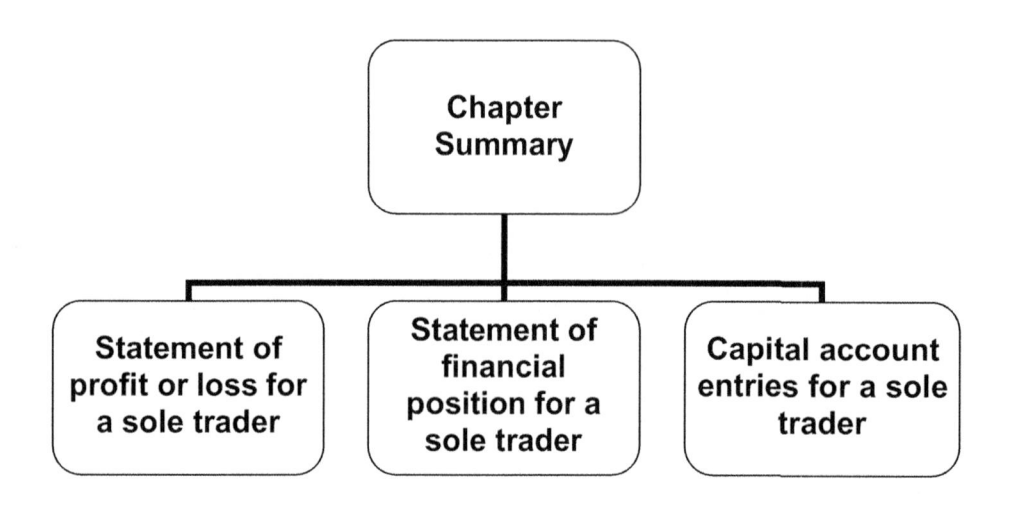

```
                    Chapter Summary
          ┌─────────────┼─────────────┐
  Statement of    Statement of    Capital account
  profit or loss  financial       entries for a sole
  for a sole      position for    trader
  trader          a sole trader
```

5.2 The elements of the final accounts

Five elements make up the final accounts of a business and these are assets, liabilities, capital (equity), income and expenses.

- Assets, liabilities and capital are presented in the statement of financial position for a business, which reports about the wealth and liquidity position of the business.
- Income and expenses are presented in the statement of profit or loss, which reports profits earned (or losses incurred) by the business.

Assets

An asset is a resource controlled by the business, as a result of past events and from which future economic benefits (money) are expected to flow to the business.

Non-current assets are assets consumed or used by a business, beyond a period of one year, they are long-term investments that are used to generate products, services or cash for the business.

Examples of non-current assets

- Land and buildings.
- Manufacturing plant and equipment.
- Equipment and tools.
- Computer equipment.
- Office equipment.
- Furniture, fixtures and fittings.
- Motor vehicles.

Current assets are assets expected to be converted quickly into cash, within a period of less than one year.

Examples of current assets

- Closing inventory (purchased goods held for resale).
- Trade receivables (money owed by credit customers), also called the sales ledger control account.
- Prepaid expenses (expenses paid but not consumed in the accounting period).
- VAT owed from HMRC (more VAT reclaimed rather than paid to HMRC).
- Money in the bank account.
- Cash in hand (physical notes and coins).

Liabilities

A liability is a present obligation of the business, arising from past events, the settlement is expected to result in an outflow of economic benefits (money) from the business.

Non-current liabilities are obligations expected to be settled by the business, over a period of beyond one year.

Examples of non-current liabilities

- Bank loans.
- Hire purchase agreements.
- Lease agreements.

Current liabilities are obligations expected to be settled by the business, within a period of less than one year.

Examples of current liabilities

- VAT owed to HMRC (more VAT paid to HMRC rather than reclaimed).
- Wages owed to staff.
- Accrued expenses (expenses consumed but not paid in the accounting period).
- Bank overdraft (money owed to the bank).
- Trade payables (money owed to credit suppliers), also called the purchases ledger control account.

Capital

Capital simply means the value of ownership. It is the residual interest (whatever is left) from the assets of the business after deducting all the liabilities of the business. Total assets less total liabilities represent what is owed by the business to the owner (capital) and this amount is also called 'net assets'.

A drawings account keeps a separate record for money taken by the owner from the business, it is an account kept separate from the capital account, to provide more information.

A sole traders capital account increases, whenever the business makes more profits and decreases, whenever the owner withdraws money from the business for personal use (drawings).

Assets, liabilities and capital are presented in the statement of financial position for a business, which reports about the wealth and liquidity position of the business.

Income

Income is money earned or received by the business from the sale of goods or services, or from other income sources.

- Cash sales (sales not on credit).
- Credit sales (sales on credit).
- Rent received from the rental of premises owned by the business.
- Bank interest received.
- Discounts received for earlier settlement of purchases invoices to suppliers.
- Commission received.
- Gain on disposal of non-current assets.

Expenses

Expenses are costs incurred or paid for by the business in the normal course of trade. The cost of goods sold and other related expenses, must be matched to sales income earned in the same accounting period.

- Cash purchases (purchases not on credit).
- Credit purchases (purchases on credit).
- Carriage inwards (delivery costs for goods delivered by suppliers).
- Carriage outwards (delivery costs for goods delivered to customers).
- Rent, insurance and heating for business premises.
- Staff wages.
- Motor vehicle expenses such as fuel, insurance, servicing and repairs.
- Advertising costs.
- Depreciation charges (cost for the wear and tear of non-current assets).
- Bank interest and charges.
- Loan interest.
- Discounts allowed for earlier settlement of sales invoices by credit customers.
- Accountancy and legal services.
- Loss on disposal of non-current assets.
- Irrecoverable debts written off.

Income and expenses are presented in the statement of profit or loss, which report profits earned (or losses incurred) by the business. The statement of profit or loss shows how well the business is performing. Any profits earned is owed to the owner of the business (increasing the capital balance) and any losses incurred, reduce what is owed to the owner of the business (decreasing the capital balance).

5.3 The trial balance

A 'trial balance' (a 'trial of balances') as the name suggests is an accounting statement where all debit and credit balances from the general ledger (a double-entry system) are shown together to test their equality. A trial balance is prepared to check the arithmetical accuracy of accounting entries that have been made and to prepare the final accounts of the business.

Exam tasks may expect you to prepare final accounts for a sole trader and a trial balance will be provided for you to complete the exam task. The trial balance will have a green highlighter feature in the task, to highlight trial balance figures, this will be useful to ensure you have not missed any figures you have entered in the task layout provided.

Exam tasks may expect:

- A statement of profit or loss prepared for a sole trader in a given layout (format), itemise income and expenditure and transfer data from the trial balance to the appropriate line of the statement of profit or loss, in line with given information about organisational policies.
- A statement of financial position prepared for a sole trader in a 'net assets' layout (format) and transfer of data from the trial balance to the appropriate line of the statement of financial position.

DEAD CLIC

Don't get clouded in the double entry logic, ledgers are just balances kept for the five elements of the final accounts and we are either increasing or decreasing these balances according to the rules of double entry.

DEAD CLIC is an acronym that defines the elements of final accounts and indicates whether each element would be overall a debit, or credit balance. It can also be used to determine the correct double entry to increase or decrease a ledger account balance, providing the element is known.

DEAD CLIC

Debit	**C**redit
Expenses	**L**iabilities
Assets	**I**ncome
Drawings	**C**apital

The elements	Natural state	Increase balance (as per the natural state)	Decrease balance (opposite to natural state)
Income	Credit	Credit	Debit
Expenses	Debit	Debit	Credit
Assets	Debit	Debit	Credit
Liabilities	Credit	Credit	Debit
Capital	Credit	Credit	Debit

Practice example

A trial balance for a business has been prepared. Identify whether each element is income, expenses, assets, liabilities, capital or drawings.

Trial balance as at 30 April 20X8

	DR £	CR £	Element
Office equipment at cost	18000		
Motor vehicles at cost	14500		
Depreciation charges	8000		
Accumulated depreciation - office equipment		4500	
Accumulated depreciation - motor vehicles		3500	
Opening inventory	5500		
Cash at bank	14600		
Sales ledger control account	22300		
Sales		98500	
Sales returns	2400		
Discounts allowed	5560		
Irrecoverable debts	5000		
HMRC liability		1500	
VAT owing to HM Customs and Revenue		5410	
Purchase ledger control account		13400	
Discounts received		500	
Purchase returns		3250	
Closing inventory	4100	4100	
Purchases	26900		
Capital		49880	
Drawings	24000		
Light and heat	1870		
Interest received		650	
Advertising	3000		
Telephone expenses	1340		
Motor vehicle expenses	5920		
Staff wages	10200		
Rent paid	12000		
TOTAL	185190	185190	

The solution is shown on the next page.

Solution to practice example

Trial balance as at 30 April 20X8

	DR £	CR £	Element
Office equipment at cost	18000		Asset
Motor vehicles at cost	14500		Asset
Depreciation charges	8000		Expense
Accumulated depreciation - office equipment		4500	Contra asset
Accumulated depreciation - motor vehicles		3500	Contra asset
Opening inventory	5500		Expense
Cash at bank	14600		Asset
Sales ledger control account	22300		Asset
Sales		98500	Income
Sales returns	2400		Expense
Discounts allowed	5560		Expense
Irrecoverable debts	5000		Expense
HMRC liability		1500	Liability
VAT owing to HM Customs and Revenue		5410	Liability
Purchase ledger control account		13400	Liability
Discounts received		500	Income
Purchase returns		3250	Income
Closing inventory	4100	4100	Asset/Expense
Purchases	26900		Expense
Capital		49880	Capital
Drawings	24000		Drawings
Light and heat	1870		Expense
Interest received		650	Income
Advertising	3000		Expense
Telephone expenses	1340		Expense
Motor vehicle expenses	5920		Expense
Staff wages	10200		Expense
Rent paid	12000		Expense
TOTAL	**185190**	**185190**	

Cash at bank was a debit balance (an asset) in the trial balance, alternatively a bank overdraft could exist and if so would be a credit balance (a liability).

HMRC liability in the trial balance represents income tax and national insurance owed from staff wages paid by the business. VAT in the trial balance was owed by the business to HMRC, which is a current liability, alternatively a task could include VAT owed from HMRC as a current asset, which would be a debit (not credit) balance.

Sales returns may alternatively be viewed as a reduction (contra) against sales income for the accounting year. The 'debit' for sales returns (credit notes) can reduce sales income (invoices), which is a 'credit' balance, rather than be treated as an expense. In any event sales returns are a debit balance. Exam tasks will normally expect you to include sales as one single figure in the trading account of a statement of profit or loss, after deducting sales returns.

Purchases returns may alternatively be viewed as a reduction (contra) against purchases for the accounting year. The 'credit' for purchases returns (credit notes) can reduce purchases (invoices), which is a 'debit' balance, rather than be treated as income. In any event purchases returns are a credit balance. Exam tasks will normally expect you to include purchases as one single figure in the trading account of a statement of profit or loss, after deducting purchases returns.

Trial balance figures may also include carriage inwards and carriage outwards. Carriage refers to the cost of transporting goods to and from the business.

Carriage inwards represents an expense for delivery charges made by suppliers and is normally treated as part of the cost of goods sold. Exam tasks will normally expect you to include purchases as one single figure in the trading account of a statement of profit or loss, after adding carriage inwards and deducting purchases returns.

Carriage outwards represents delivery charges incurred by the business to transport goods sold to its customers, this expense is included with other expenses below the trading account of a statement of profit or loss.

Opening inventory is a debit balance (expense) which is added to purchases in the trading account of a statement of profit or loss. Closing inventory represents the cost of unsold goods (purchases) for the period. The trial balance will include the closing inventory figure twice, the debit balance is for closing inventory presented as a current asset, owned by the business and the credit balance, is to reduce the cost of goods sold in the trading account of a statement of profit or loss.

Non-current assets

The double entry to record depreciation is to debit depreciation charges (increase expenses in the statement of profit or loss account) and credit accumulated depreciation (decrease the value of the non-current asset held in the statement of financial position).

Non-current assets are recorded at original cost which would be a debit balance (asset) and accumulated depreciation is kept separately as a credit balance. Both accounts are presented together in the statement of financial position. The original cost less the accumulated depreciation is called the carrying value of the asset. Accumulated depreciation (a credit balance) is often referred to as a 'contra asset account' because it is netted off against original cost (a debit balance), to calculate the carrying value of a non-current asset.

Irrecoverable debts

When a specific customer account is identified as 'uncollectible' (irrecoverable) then irrecoverable debts expenses are written off the statement of profit or loss.

Allowances for doubtful debts

An allowance for doubtful debts is made when the recoverability of a customer balance is 'doubtful' or 'uncertain', but definitely 'not irrecoverable'. A doubtful debt is a debt that is 'unlikely to be paid', rather than 'definitely will not be paid'.

The allowance for doubtful debts would be a credit balance and shown in the statement of financial position, it represents the amount for doubtful debts that has been provided for against trade receivables. It is not a liability because it does not represent an obligation to pay a third party. The credit balance is often referred to as a 'contra asset' account, because it is netted off against the debit balance of trade receivables in the statement of financial position. Exam tasks will normally expect you to include trade receivables as one single figure after deducting the allowance for doubtful debts.

The allowance for doubtful debts can increase or decrease for each accounting period. The increase or decrease is included in the statement of profit or loss and is called an 'allowance for doubtful debts: adjustment'. The amount can be a debit or credit balance and is shown in the statement of profit or loss. A debit balance increases expenses in the statement of profit or loss. A credit balance decreases expenses in the statement of profit or loss (shown as a negative figure which reduces expenses).

5.4 Final accounts for a sole trader

Practice example

This task is about final accounts for a sole trader and a trial balance is shown below.

- Sales revenue should include sales returns.
- Purchases should include purchase returns.
- If necessary, use a minus sign to indicate ONLY the deduction of an account balance used to make up costs of goods sold, or a loss for the year.

Trial balance as at 30 April 20X8

	DR £	CR £
Office equipment at cost	18000	
Motor vehicles at cost	14500	
Depreciation charges	8000	
Accumulated depreciation - office equipment		4500
Accumulated depreciation - motor vehicles		3500
Opening inventory	5500	
Cash at bank	14600	
Sales ledger control account	22300	
Sales		98500
Sales returns	2400	
Discounts allowed	5560	
Irrecoverable debts	5000	
HMRC liability		1500
VAT owing to HM Customs and Revenue		5410
Purchase ledger control account		13400
Discounts received		500
Purchase returns		3250
Closing inventory	4100	4100
Purchases	26900	
Capital		49880
Drawings	24000	
Light and heat	1870	
Interest received		650
Advertising	3000	
Telephone expenses	1340	
Motor vehicle expenses	5920	
Staff wages	10200	
Rent paid	12000	
TOTAL	**185190**	**185190**

Picklist: Opening inventory, Purchases, Closing inventory, Discounts received, Interest received, Depreciation charges, Discounts allowed, Irrecoverable debts, Light and heat, Advertising, Telephone expenses, Motor vehicle expenses, Staff wages, Rent, Opening capital, Profit for the year, Loss for the year, Drawings, Closing capital, Office equipment, Motor vehicles, Trade receivables, Cash at bank, HMRC liability, VAT owed to HMRC, Trade payables.

Statement of profit or loss for the year ended 30 April 20X8

	£	£
Sales revenue		
Cost of goods sold		
Gross profit		
Add:		
Less:		
Total expenses		
Net profit or loss		

Statement of financial position as at 30 April 20X8

	Cost £	Accumulated depreciation £	Carrying amount £
Non-current assets			
Current assets			
Current liabilities			
Net current assets			
Net assets			
Financed by			

The solution is shown on the next page.

Solution to practice example

Statement of profit or loss for the year ended 30 April 20X8

	£	£
Sales revenue (£98,500 - £2,400)		96,100
Opening inventory	5,500	
Purchases (£26,900 - £3,250)	23,650	
Closing inventory	-4,100	
Cost of goods sold		25,050
Gross profit		71,050
Add:		
Discounts received	500	
Interest received	650	
		1,150
Less:		
Depreciation charges	8,000	
Discounts allowed	5,560	
Irrecoverable debts	5,000	
Light and heat	1,870	
Advertising	3,000	
Telephone expenses	1,340	
Motor vehicle expenses	5,920	
Staff wages	10,200	
Rent	12,000	
Total expenses		52,890
Net profit or loss		19,310

Statement of financial position as at 30 April 20X8

	Cost £	Accumulated depreciation £	Carrying amount £
Non-current assets			
Office equipment	18,000	4,500	13,500
Motor vehicles	14,500	3,500	11,000
			24,500
Current assets			
Closing inventory		4,100	
Trade receivables		22,300	
Cash at bank		14,600	
		41,000	
Current liabilities			
HMRC liability	1,500		
VAT owed to HMRC	5,410		
Trade payables	13,400		
		20,310	
Net current assets			20,690
Net assets			45,190
Financed by			
Opening capital			49,880
Add: Profit for the year			19,310
Less: Drawings			24,000
Closing capital			45,190

Exam tasks will use the 'net assets' layout (see above) for the statement of financial position. The statement of financial position can also be referred to as a 'balance sheet' because net assets (£45,190) should be equal to closing capital (£45,190) and therefore both figures should balance. The statement shown above is a picture or snapshot of the financial position of a business as at 30 April 20X8.

Exam tasks will expect you to distinguish between non-current assets and current assets in a statement of financial position. Non-current assets use the column titles provided at the top of the statement of financial position.

	Cost £	Accumulated depreciation £	Carrying amount £
Non-current assets			
Office equipment	18,000	4,500	13,500
Motor vehicles	14,500	3,500	11,000
			24,500

Each type of non-current asset will have its cost (debit) and accumulated depreciation (credit) balance included in the statement of financial position. The carrying value is also included (cost - accumulated depreciation) for each type of non-current asset. The total carrying value of non-current assets (£24,500) is the figure that is added to 'net current assets' (£20,690) to calculate 'net assets' (£45,190).

Current assets (£41,000) and current liabilities (£20,310) are offset and the final figure is presented as 'net current assets' (£20,690) in the statement of financial position.

Net profit earned by the business for the year (£19,310) is added to the opening capital account balance of the owner in the statement of financial position. The double entry would be to credit (increase) capital (£19,310) and to debit the profit or loss account (£19,310) for the year ended (to close down the profit or loss account).

Drawings (£24,000) are deducted from the opening capital account balance of the owner in the statement of financial position. Net assets are £45,190 and this figure should be equal to the closing capital account balance of the owner.

The accounting equation

Total Assets (Debit) - Total Liabilities (Credit) = Capital (Credit).

The accounting equation states that total assets less total liabilities (net assets) would be equal to capital, owed by the business to the owner. The statement of financial position uses the same logic as the accounting equation.

5.5 The capital account

The separate entity concept states as a rule that the transactions of a business and the private transactions of the owner are recorded separately for accounting purposes. In substance (not legal form) the business and the sole trader are treated as two separate people for accounting purposes. The capital account records the private transactions of the owner such as, the money they have invested in the business or the drawings they have taken from the business.

From the previous example, final accounts were prepared for a sole trader and the statement of financial position showed the following movements for the capital account.

Financed by	£
Opening capital	49,880
Add: Profit for the year	19,310
Less: Drawings	24,000
Closing capital	45,190

Exam tasks may expect you to complete capital account ledger entries for a sole trader. The above entries are included in the capital account shown below.

Capital account

Details	Amount £	Details	Amount £
Drawings	24,000	Balance b/d	49,880
Balance c/d	45,190	Profit or loss account	19,310
Total	69,190	Total	69,190
		Balance b/d	45,190

The natural state of a capital account is a credit balance, because the business owes this amount to the owner. The balance b/d at the beginning of the year was £49,880 (credit).

Net profits earned by the business are owed to the owner. A credit of £19,310 is made which increases the capital account balance owed to the owner. The double entry would be to debit the profit or loss account with £19,310 (to close this account for the year) and to credit the capital account with £19,310. When the business makes money, then the owner also makes money and their capital account balance will increase.

If the business had incurred a net loss for the year, the double entry would be the opposite, to debit (decrease) the capital account and credit the profit or loss account (to close this account for the year). When the business loses money, then the owner also loses money and their capital account balance will decrease.

The drawings account is kept as a separate record for money taken personally by the owner of the business. The natural state of a drawings account is a debit balance. The drawings account is closed at the end of each accounting year and the amount posted to the capital account. The double entry shown above would be to debit (decrease) the capital account with £24,000 and to credit the drawings account with £24,000 (to close this account for the year).

The capital account is totalled and balanced at the end of the accounting year and the balance c/d is £45,190.

Other capital account entries:

- Cash invested by the owner.

DR   Bank (increase assets).
CR   Capital (increase capital).

- Motor vehicle (or other non-current assets) introduced by the owner.

DR   Motor vehicle (increase assets).
CR   Capital (increase capital).

- Goods for resale introduced by the owner.

DR   Purchases (increase expenses).
CR   Capital (increase capital).

- Business motor vehicle expenses (or other expenses) paid for by the owner.

DR   Motor vehicle expenses (increase expenses).
CR   Capital (increase capital).

In all the examples above, the double entry would be to CREDIT (increase) capital.

Drawings

The drawings account records money, goods or assets taken personally by the owner from the business.

Examples of drawings

- Cash withdrawn by the owner for personal use.
- Assets taken by the owner for personal use e.g. vehicles, equipment or tools.
- Goods for resale (purchases) taken by the owner for personal use.
- Private expenses of the owner that are paid by the business e.g. personal telephone bills or motor expenses.

Drawings account entries:

- Cash taken from the business bank account by the owner.

DR   Drawings (increase drawings).
CR   Bank (decrease asset).

- Business motor vehicle (or other non-current assets) taken by the owner.

DR   Drawings (increase drawings).
CR   Motor vehicle (decrease asset).

- Business goods for resale (purchases) taken by the owner.

DR   Drawings (increase drawings).
CR   Purchases (decrease expenses).

- Private expenses of the owner that are paid by the business.

DR   Drawings (increase drawings).
CR   Expenses (decrease expenses).

In all the examples above, the double entry would be to DEBIT (increase) drawings.

- The drawings account is closed at the end of the accounting year.

DR   Capital (decrease capital).
CR   Drawings (decrease drawings).

Chapter activities

Activity 5.1

This task is about final accounts for a sole trader and a trial balance is shown below.

The following accounting policies are used by the business:

- Sales revenue should include sales returns, if any.
- Purchases should include purchase returns and carriage inwards, if any.
- Trade receivables are shown net of any allowance for doubtful debts.

Prepare a statement of profit or loss for the year ended 30 June 20X3 and a statement of financial position as at 30 June 20X3. If necessary, use a minus sign to indicate ONLY the following:

- **the deduction of an account balance used to make up costs of goods sold.**
- **a loss for the year.**

Trial balance as at 30 June 20X3

	DR £	CR £
Fixtures and fittings at cost	18,000	
Depreciation charges	4,500	
Accumulated depreciation - Fixtures and fittings		9,000
Allowance for doubtful debts		310
Opening inventory	12,300	
Bank overdraft		1,450
Trade receivables	15,600	
Sales		58,900
Sales returns	800	
Irrecoverable debts	400	
Allowance for doubtful debts - adjustment	60	
VAT owed to HMRC		4,320
Trade payables		7,830
Carriage outwards	790	
Carriage inwards	540	
Purchase returns		250
Closing inventory	11,100	11,100
Purchases	18,900	
Capital		24,020
Drawings	12,000	
Bank interest and charges	340	
Premises expenses	9,000	
Telephone expenses	2,900	
Staff wages	9,200	
Prepaid expenses	750	
TOTAL	**117,180**	**117,180**

Picklist: Fixtures and fittings, Trade receivables, Prepayments, Bank overdraft, Trade payables, VAT owed to HMRC, Opening capital, Profit for the year, Loss for the year, Drawings, Closing capital, Opening inventory, Purchases, Closing inventory, Depreciation charges, Irrecoverable debts, Allowance for doubtful debts - adjustment, Carriage outwards, Bank interest and charges, Premises expenses, Telephone expenses, Staff wages.

Statement of profit or loss for the year ended 30 June 20X3

	£	£
Sales revenue		
▼		
▼		
▼		
▼		
Cost of goods sold		
Gross profit		
Add:		
▼		
▼		
▼		
Less:		
▼		
▼		
▼		
▼		
▼		
▼		
▼		
▼		
▼		
▼		
Total expenses		
Net profit or loss		

Statement of financial position as at 30 June 20X3

	Cost £	Accumulated depreciation £	Carrying amount £
Non-current assets			
Current assets			
Current liabilities			
Net current assets			
Net assets			
Financed by			

Activity 5.2

This task is about final accounts for a sole trader and a trial balance is shown below.

The following accounting policies are used by the business:
- Sales revenue should include sales returns, if any.
- Purchases should include purchase returns and carriage inwards, if any.
- Trade receivables are shown net of any allowance for doubtful debts.

Prepare a statement of profit or loss for the year ended 31 August 20X8 and a statement of financial position as at 31 August 20X8. If necessary, use a minus sign to indicate ONLY the following:
- **the deduction of an account balance used to make up costs of goods sold.**
- **a decrease in allowance for doubtful debts - adjustment.**
- **a loss for the year.**

Trial balance as at 31 August 20X8

	DR £	CR £
Motor vehicles at cost	25,000	
Depreciation charges	5,000	
Accumulated depreciation - Motor vehicles		10,000
Allowance for doubtful debts		200
Opening inventory	5,000	
Bank	7,620	
Sales ledger control account	2,500	
Sales		34,200
Sales returns	2,800	
Irrecoverable debts	1,000	
Allowance for doubtful debts - adjustment		120
VAT owing from HMRC	1,240	
Purchase ledger control account		5,490
Closing inventory	5,500	5,500
Purchases	19,500	
Capital		50,300
Drawings	20,500	
Interest received		250
Advertising	5,000	
Telephone expenses	2,900	
Motor vehicle expenses	4,500	
Accruals		2,000
TOTAL	**108,060**	**108,060**

Picklist: Motor vehicles, Trade receivables, Accruals, Bank, Trade payables, VAT owing from HMRC, Opening capital, Profit for the year, Loss for the year, Drawings, Closing capital, Opening inventory, Purchases, Closing inventory, Depreciation charges, Irrecoverable debts, Allowance for doubtful debts - adjustment, Interest received, Motor vehicle expenses, Advertising, Telephone expenses, Staff wages.

Statement of financial position as at 31 August 20X8

	Cost £	Accumulated depreciation £	Carrying amount £
Non-current assets			
⇩			
Current assets			
⇩			
⇩			
⇩			
⇩			
⇩			
Current liabilities			
⇩			
⇩			
⇩			
⇩			
⇩			
⇩			
Net current assets			
Net assets			
Financed by			
⇩			
⇩			
⇩			
⇩			

Statement of profit or loss for the year ended 31 August 20X8

	£	£
Sales revenue		
Cost of goods sold		
Gross profit		
Add:		
Less:		
Total expenses		
Net profit or loss		

Activity 5.3

A sole trader started in business on the 1 November 20X7.

- The sole trader introduced £10,000 cash into the business and their own personal motor vehicle worth £7,500.
- Profit for the year ended 31 October 20X8 was £14,230.

Complete the capital account for the year ended 31 October 20X8. Show clearly the balance carried down to the next financial year.

Picklist: Balance b/d, Balance c/d, Bank, Capital, Drawings, Motor vehicles, Motor vehicle expenses, Profit or loss account.

Capital account

	£		£

Activity 5.4

Indicate for each transaction below whether it would be a debit entry, or credit entry, or no posting made to the capital account of a sole trader, in the general ledger. Choose ONE answer for each transaction below.

	Debit	Credit	No posting
Drawings for the year ended	☐	☐	☐
A loss for the year ended	☐	☐	☐
Payment of business expenses through the business bank account	☐	☐	☐
A personal motor vehicle introduced by the owner	☐	☐	☐

Activity 5.5

Use drag and drop to shown the correct double entry if business goods for resale are taken for personal use by the owner of the business.

Options	Debit	Credit
Purchases returns		
Capital		
Purchases		
Drawings		

Debit: Drawings
Credit: Purchases

Activity 5.6

The following information is for a sole trader for the year ended 31 August 20X2.

- The net assets of the business on 1 September 20X1 was £34,900.
- The business incurred a loss of £12,510 for the year ended 31 August 20X2.
- The sole trader withdrew £16,000 during the year as drawings from the business bank account.

Complete the capital account for the year ended 31 August 20X2. Show clearly the balance carried down to the next financial year.

Picklist: Balance b/d, Balance c/d, Capital, Drawings, Profit or loss account.

Capital account

	£		£

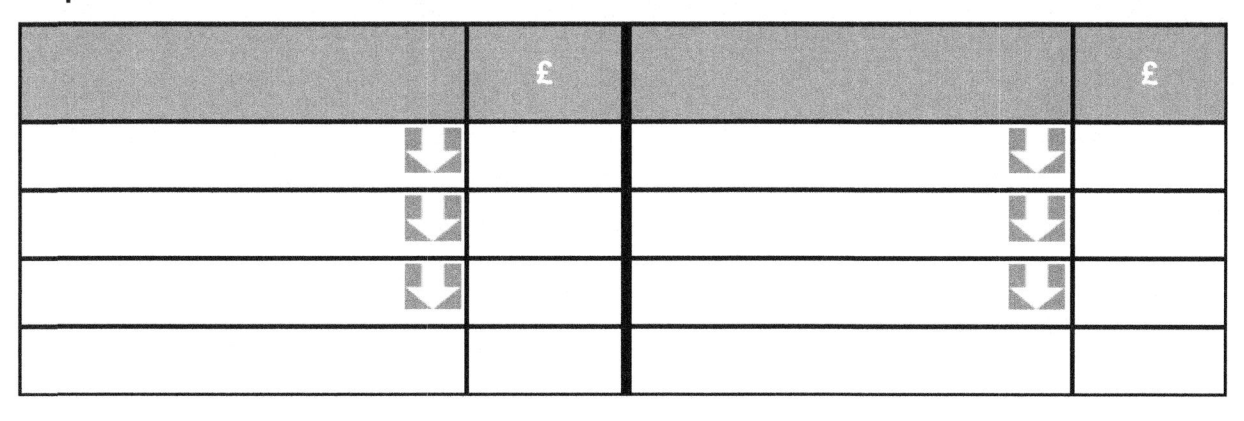

End of Task

6 Preparing Accounts for Partnerships

6.1 Introduction

This chapter will explain the key components of partnership accounts.

- Prepare a statement of profit or loss.
- Prepare a partnership appropriation account.
- The nature and content of partners' current accounts.
- The nature and content of partners' capital accounts.
- Prepare a statement of financial position.

The following points will apply to exam tasks:

- The number of partners will be limited to a maximum of three.
- There will be no changes in the partnership during an accounting year.
- Either a profit or loss may be provided for allocation between partners.

This chapter covers final accounts for unincorporated partnerships, not Limited Liability Partnerships (LLP). An LLP is formed through the process of legal incorporation, like a company. Accounting standards regulate and govern extensively how LLP financial statements should be prepared and presented.

The statement of profit or loss and financial position was covered in chapter 5.

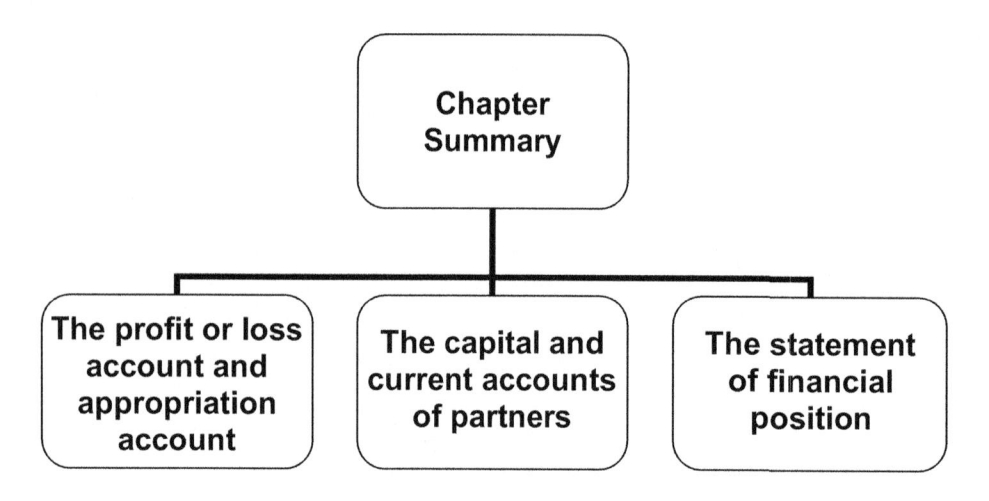

Chapter Summary

- The profit or loss account and appropriation account
- The capital and current accounts of partners
- The statement of financial position

6.2 The key components of a partnership agreement

A partnership is when two or more self-employed persons run a business together, with a common view to earn profits.

- Profits earned by the business will be shared (allocated) between partners.
- Partners pay income tax and national insurance on their share of profits from the partnership business.

It is advisable to have a partnership agreement that sets out the rights, duties and obligations for each partner.

A partnership agreement may typically contain:

- Percentage ownership of business net assets (capital) for each partner.
- Salary entitlement for each partner.
- Sales commission entitlement for each partner.
- Interest on capital invested for each partner.
- Interest on drawings charged to each partner for money taken from the business.
- How residual profits or losses will be shared (ratio, fraction or percentage).
- The length of the partnership agreement.
- Roles, responsibilities and authority levels of each partner.
- How disputes and conflicts will be resolved.
- What happens if there is withdrawal or death of a partner.

The Partnership Act 1890 defines a partnership as persons carrying on a business in common with a view of profit. Partnerships do not always have a written partnership agreement, this can create problems if disagreements, or other problems arise. If a partnership agreement does not exist, the Partnership Act 1890 is applied as the rule of law for any civil disputes in a partnership.

Partnership Act 1890 (applied if no partnership agreement)

- Profits or losses will be shared equally.
- No partner is entitled to a salary.
- No partner is entitled to receive interest on capital.
- No partner will be charged interest on drawings.
- If a partner has contributed more capital 'than agreed', they are entitled to receive 5% interest per annum, on the 'excess capital' they have contributed.

Why a formal partnership agreement may not exist

- Partners may want profits or losses to be shared equally and this is what the law would prescribe.
- Partners initially may wish to keep things informal, especially when starting the business for the first time, an agreement may be drawn up later, when each partner gets a feel for how the business will work.

6.3 Preparing a partnership appropriation account

A statement of profit or loss account for a partnership is prepared in exactly the same way as a sole trader. The main purpose of an appropriation account is to show how profits or losses, from the statement of profit or loss account, is shared (allocated) amongst the partners in a partnership.

A sole trader does not need to prepare an appropriation account, because 100% of all profits or losses earned by the business belong wholly to the sole trader. A partnership does need to prepare an appropriation account, because profits or losses need to be shared according to the terms of the partnership agreement.

Example of a partnership appropriation account

	£
Profit or loss for appropriation	
Add:	
Interest on drawings – A	
Interest on drawings – B	
Deduct:	
Interest on capital – A	
Interest on capital – B	
Salary – A	
Salary – B	
Sales commission – A	
Sales commission – B	
Residual profit or loss available for distribution	
Share of residual profit or loss:	
Share of residual profit or loss – A	
Share of residual profit loss – B	
Total residual profit or loss distributed	

The profit or loss for appropriation would be the net profit or net loss figure taken from the statement of profit or loss.

Interest of drawings

Partners maybe penalised for taking drawings from the business, interest on drawings maybe charged to each partner and the amounts added to the net profit or loss for appropriation. If a partner takes more drawings, then ultimately, they will be charged more interest, this acts as a disincentive for partners to take too much money from the business. Exam tasks will not expect you to calculate interest on drawings, but you must be able to account for it when preparing an appropriation account.

Interest of capital

Partners maybe allocated interest on their capital invested in the partnership business, so if partner invests more capital, they will be allocated more interest. This acts as an incentive for partners to keep and invest their money in the partnership business. Interest on capital is deducted from the net profit or loss for appropriation. Exam tasks will not expect you to calculate interest on capital, but you must be able to account for it when preparing an appropriation account.

Salaries

If a partner works more hours than other partners, or has more expertise or skills, they may be allocated a salary. Salaries are deducted from the net profit or loss for appropriation.

Sales commission

Partners maybe entitled to sales commission on their sales results achieved for the business. Sales commission incentivises and motivates partners to worker harder to sell more goods and achieve higher sales results. Sales commission is deducted from the net profit or loss for appropriation.

The residual profit or loss

The net profit or loss is adjusted for salaries, sales commission, interest on drawings and interest on capital, to calculate the residual profit or loss. Residual means whatever is remaining. The residual profit or loss will be shared according to the profit or loss sharing agreement for each partner.

It is very unlikely an exam task would require every entry above to be included in an appropriation account. The exam task would explain the terms of the partnership agreement and provide the net profit or loss figure from the statement of profit or loss.

Practice example

You have been given the following trial balance for a partnership business.

The partners are Anne and Burt.

The following accounting policies are used by the business:
- Sales revenue should include sales returns, if any.
- Purchases should include purchase returns and carriage inwards, if any.

Trial balance as at 31 March 20X5

	DR £	CR £
Office equipment - at cost	18000	
Motor vehicles - at cost	14500	
Depreciation charges	8000	
Accumulated depreciation - office equipment		4500
Accumulated depreciation - motor vehicles		3500
Opening inventory	5500	
Cash at bank	14600	
Sales ledger control account	22300	
Sales		124350
Sales returns	2400	
Discounts allowed	5560	
Irrecoverable debts	5000	
HMRC liability		1500
VAT owing to HMRC		5410
Purchase ledger control account		13400
Discounts received		500
Purchase returns		3250
Closing inventory	4100	4100
Purchases	26900	
Capital - Anne		15000
Capital - Burt		10000
Current - Anne		9450
Current - Burt	2420	
Drawings - Anne	20000	
Drawings - Burt	12000	
Light and heat	1870	
Interest received		650
Advertising	3000	
Telephone expenses	1340	
Motor vehicle expenses	5920	
Staff wages	10200	
Rent	12000	
TOTAL	**195610**	**195610**

A statement of profit or loss is prepared in exactly the same way for a sole trader.

Statement of profit or loss for the year ended 31 March 20X5

	£	£
Sales revenue (£124,350 - £2,400)		121,950
Opening inventory	5,500	
Purchases (£26,900 - £3,250)	23,650	
Closing inventory	-4,100	
Cost of goods sold		25,050
Gross profit		96,900
Add:		
Discounts received	500	
Interest received	650	
		1,150
Less:		
Depreciation charges	8,000	
Discounts allowed	5,560	
Irrecoverable debts	5,000	
Light and heat	1,870	
Advertising	3,000	
Telephone expenses	1,340	
Motor vehicle expenses	5,920	
Staff wages	10,200	
Rent	12,000	
Total expenses		52,890
Net profit		45,160

The net profit relating to the year ended 31 March 20X5 was £45,160.

The terms of the partnership agreement between Anne and Burt are as follows:

	Anne	**Burt**
Share of profit or loss	60%	40%
Salary (per month)	0	£500
Sales commission earned for the year	£3,450	£2,900
Interest on capital	£1,500	£1,000
Interest on drawings	£1,000	£600

Partnership appropriation account for the year ended 31 March 20X5

	£
Profit or loss for appropriation	45,160
Add:	
Interest on drawings – A	1,000
Interest on drawings – B	600
Deduct:	
Interest on capital – A	-1,500
Interest on capital – B	-1,000
Salary – A	0
Salary – B (£500 x 12 months)	-6,000
Sales commission – A	-3,450
Sales commission – B	-2,900
Residual profit or loss available for distribution	31,910
Share of residual profit or loss:	
Share of residual profit or loss – A (£31,910 ÷ 100% x 60%)	19,146
Share of residual profit loss – B (£31,910 ÷ 100% x 40%)	12,764
Total residual profit or loss distributed	31,910

- The appropriation account begins with the net profit of £45,160 from the statement of profit or loss.
- Interest on drawings are added to the net profit of £45,160.
- Salary, sales commission and interest on capital are deducted from the net profit of £45,160. It is normal for exam tasks to require inclusion of zero figures for example, Anne's salary information (zero) is still included.
- Once all the above has been allocated to each partner, the residual profit available for distribution (whatever remains) is £31,910. This amount is distributed to each partner based on each partners' share of profit or loss agreed. Anne is entitled to a 60% share and Burt is entitled to a 40% share.
- Minus signs for an appropriation account (see above) are normally used in exam tasks, for any deductions made from net profit or loss, or when there is a loss.

Ratios, fractions and percentages

The share of profit or loss between partners can be expressed as a ratio, fraction or percentage.

The share of profit or loss between Anne and Burt as a percentage was 60% and 40% respectively. The residual profit available for distribution was £31,910 (100%) which means that Anne is entitled to £19,146 (£31,910 ÷ 100% x 60%) and Burt is entitled to £12,764 (£31,910 ÷ 100% x 40%).

The share of profit or loss between Anne and Burt as a fraction, would be 3/5 (three fifths) and 2/5 (fifths) respectively. The residual profit available for distribution was £31,910 which means that Anne is entitled to £19,146 (£31,910 ÷ 5 x 3) and Burt is entitled to £12,764 (£31,910 ÷ 5 x 2).

The share of profit or loss between Anne and Burt as a ratio, would be 3:2 respectively. The residual profit available for distribution was £31,910 which means that Anne is entitled to £19,146 (£31,910 ÷ (3 + 2) x 3) and Burt is entitled to £12,764 (£31,910 ÷ (3 + 2) x 2).

6.4 Capital and current accounts

Partnerships offer many benefits, in particular more capital invested, skills and expertise contributed and others to share the responsibilities of running a business. However, the liability of partners for the debts of the business is unlimited which can be a significant risk to each partner.

The separate entity concept states as a rule that the transactions of a business and the private transactions of its owners, are treated as two separate people for accounting purposes. Partners would normally keep two accounts for private transactions, which is a capital account and current account.

Capital account

Capital accounts record the permanent (fixed) capital that is invested in the business by each partner. To protect against the starvation of the business from excessive drawings made by each partner, capital accounts are normally 'protected' and each partner would need consent from the other partners to make drawings from this account. The balance for a capital account should be in credit, it represents money invested by each partner that is owed by the business.

A sole trader only needs to keep a capital account to record their profits (or losses) and drawings taken for each accounting year, this is because 100% of the net assets of the business belong wholly to the sole trader.

Current account

Current accounts record the current balance that each partner can draw from the business at any time they choose. The balance of current accounts will fluctuate from year to year and are kept separate from the capital accounts of each partner.

The balance for a current account should be in credit, but can also be overdrawn (in debit), this can happen if partners have taken more drawings out of the business than their share of profits allocated.

- The partnership appropriation account increases (credits) the current account balance for salaries, sales commission, interest on capital and the distribution of residual profits to a partner.
- The partnership appropriation account decreases (debits) the current account balance for interest on drawings and the distribution of residual losses to a partner.
- Drawings decreases (debits) the current account balance for each partner.

Exam tasks may expect you to prepare ledger accounting entries for current accounts and capital accounts in a partnership. You need to be able to link current account entries with the figures taken from an appropriation account.

Practice example

Prepare the current accounts for Anne and Burt for the year ended 31 March 20X5. Information from the trial balance and the appropriation account prepared earlier will be used for completing this task.

Solution to practice example

- The opening current account balances (from the trial balance) were £9,450 (credit) for Anne and £2,420 (debit) for Burt. Burt started the accounting year with an overdrawn current account balance (debit).
- Amounts are entered from the partnership appropriation account to the current account of each partner.
- Drawings (from the trial balance) are posted to the current accounts of each partner, which were £20,000 (debit) for Anne and £12,000 (debit) for Burt.
- Current accounts are totalled and balanced for the year ended and the closing balances are £12,546 (credit) for Anne and £7,644 (credit) for Burt. Neither current account is overdrawn.

Current account - Anne

Details	Amount £	Details	Amount £
Interest on drawings	1,000	Balance b/d	9,450
Drawings	20,000	Interest on capital	1,500
Balance c/d	12,546	Sales commission	3,450
		Share of profit or loss	19,146
Total	33,546	Total	33,546

Current account - Burt

Details	Amount £	Details	Amount £
Balance b/d	2,420	Interest on capital	1,000
Interest on drawings	600	Salaries	6,000
Drawings	12,000	Sales commission	2,900
Balance c/d	7,644	Share of profit or loss	12,764
Total	22,664	Total	22,664

Exam tasks may use a combined layout for all partner current accounts and an illustration for Anne and Burt is shown below. The names of each partner are included in columns for completing the debit and credit entries.

Current accounts

Details	Anne £	Burt £	Details	Anne £	Burt £
Balance b/d		2,420	Balance b/d	9,450	
Interest on drawings	1,000	600	Interest on capital	1,500	1,000
Drawings	20,000	12,000	Salaries	0	6,000
Balance c/d	12,546	7,644	Sales commission	3,450	2,900
			Share of profit or loss	19,146	12,764
Total	33,546	22,664	Total	33,546	22,664

The double entry to post from an appropriation account to a current account:

Interest on drawings and share of residual losses for the year.

- **Debit**   Current accounts (decrease balance owed to partners)
- **Credit**   Appropriation account

Interest on capital, salaries, sales commission and share of residual profits for the year.

- **Debit**   Appropriation account
- **Credit**   Current accounts (increase balance owed to partners)

REMEMBER! Drawings are not included in an appropriation account. Drawings represent money, assets or goods taken from the business by each partner and is not an appropriation of profits (or losses).

Posting drawings to current accounts.

- **Debit**   Current accounts (decrease balance owed to partners)
- **Credit**   Drawings (decrease drawings balance to close the account)

6.5 Statement of financial position

The net assets calculation in the statement of financial position of a partnership is prepared in exactly the same way as a sole trader. The only difference is how the 'financed by' section is completed for each type of business. The 'financed by' section in the statement of financial position for a partnership, shows the closing capital and closing current account balances for each partner (columns will use the names of each partner) as shown below.

- The opening capital account balances from the trial balance for Anne and Burt was £15,000 (credit) for Anne and £10,000 (credit) for Burt. These balances are unchanged for the year ended 31 March 20X5.
- The opening current account balances from the trial balance for Anne and Burt was £9,450 (credit) for Anne and £2,420 (debit) for Burt. Amounts were entered from the appropriation account to the current account of each partner. Drawings were posted to the current account of each partner. The closing current account balances are £12,546 (credit) for Anne and £7,644 (credit) for Burt.

Statement of financial position as at 31 March 20X5

	Cost £	Accumulated depreciation £	Carrying amount £
Non-current assets			
Office equipment	18,000	4,500	13,500
Motor vehicles	14,500	3,500	11,000
			24,500
Current assets			
Closing inventory		4,100	
Trade receivables		22,300	
Cash at bank		14,600	
		41,000	
Current liabilities			
HMRC liability	1,500		
VAT owed to HMRC	5,410		
Trade payables	13,400		
		20,310	
Net current assets			20,690
Net assets			45,190
Financed by	Anne	Burt	Total
Capital accounts	15,000	10,000	25,000
Current accounts	12,546	7,644	20,190
	27,546	17,644	45,190

Neither partner had an overdrawn current account (debit balance) for the year ended 31 March 20X5. An overdrawn current account is represented as a negative figure in a statement of financial position.

Summary for preparing final accounts for a partnership

1. A statement of profit or loss is prepared for a partnership in the same way as a sole trader.
2. An appropriation account is then prepared to allocate the net profit (or net loss) to each partner.
3. The current accounts for each partner are then updated using the appropriation account and each partners drawings figure for the year ended.
4. A financial position is prepared in a similar way to a sole trader. The 'financed by' section would show the closing capital and closing current account balances for each partner.

Chapter activities

Activity 6.1

You have been given the following information about a partnership business for the year ended 31 August 20X6. The partners are Charlie and David.

	Charlie	David
Share of profit or loss	Two thirds (2/3)	One third (1/3)
Salary (per year)	0	£15,000
Interest on capital	£4,000	£1,600
Drawings	£24,000	£24,000
Current account balance 1 September 20X5	£4,600 Credit	£2,350 Debit
Capital account balance 1 September 20X5	£50,000 Credit	£20,000 Credit

The statement of profit or loss account for the year ended 31 August 20X6 showed a net profit of £39,500.

(a) Prepare a partnership appropriation account for the year ended 31 August 20X6. Use a minus sign for deductions, or where there is a loss to be distributed. You must enter zeros where appropriate in order to obtain full marks.

Picklist: Interest on capital – C, Interest on capital – D, Share of residual profit or loss – C, Share of residual profit or loss – D, Drawings – C, Drawings – D, Salary – C, Salary – D.

Partnership appropriation account for the year ended 31 August 20X6

	£
Profit or loss for appropriation	
Residual profit or loss available for distribution	
Share of residual profit or loss:	
Total residual profit or loss distributed	

(b) Prepare the current accounts for each partner for the year ended 31 August 20X6. Show clearly the balances carried down. You MUST enter zeros where appropriate in order to obtain full marks. Do NOT use brackets, minus signs or dashes.

Picklist: Balance b/d, Interest on capital, Salaries, Share of profit or loss, Drawings, Balance c/d.

Current accounts

Details	Charlie £	David £	Details	Charlie £	David £
▼			▼		
▼			▼		
▼			▼		
▼			▼		
▼			▼		
Total			Total		

Activity 6.2

You have been given the following information about a partnership business for the year ended 30 April 20X5. The partners are Ben and Vera. Both partners share profits or losses equally.

	Ben	Vera
Salary (per month)	£1,000	£500
Interest on capital (per year)	£1,000	£1,500
Drawings	£18,000	£12,000
Current account balance 1 May 20X4	£1,450 Debit	£3,340 Credit
Capital account balance 1 May 20X4	£20,000 Credit	£30,000 Credit

The statement of profit or loss account for the year ended 30 April 20X5 showed a net loss of £5,500.

(a) Prepare a partnership appropriation account for the year ended 30 April 20X5. Use a minus sign for deductions, or where there is a loss to be distributed.
You must enter zeros where appropriate in order to obtain full marks.

Picklist: Interest on capital – B, Interest on capital – B, Share of residual profit or loss – B, Share of residual profit or loss – V, Drawings – B, Drawings – V, Salary – B, Salary – V.

Partnership appropriation account for the year ended 30 April 20X5

	£
Profit or loss for appropriation	
Residual profit or loss available for distribution	
Share of residual profit or loss:	
Total residual profit or loss distributed	

(b) Prepare the current accounts for each partner for the year ended 30 April 20X5. Show clearly the balances carried down. You MUST enter zeros where appropriate in order to obtain full marks. Do NOT use brackets, minus signs or dashes.

Picklist: Balance b/d, Interest on capital, Salaries, Share of profit or loss, Drawings, Balance c/d.

Current accounts

Details	Ben £	Vera £	Details	Ben £	Vera £
Total			Total		

Activity 6.3

You have been given the following information about a partnership business for the year ended 31 May 20X2. The partners are Gary and Safina. Gary and Safina share profits or losses in the ratio of 3 to 2 respectively.

	Gary	Safina
Sales commission	£12,000	£4,500
Interest on drawings	£1,500	£650
Drawings	£15,000	£6,500
Current account balance 1 June 20X1	£3,550 Credit	£6,310 Credit

The statement of profit or loss account for the year ended 31 May 20X2 showed a net profit of £11,200.

**(a) Prepare a partnership appropriation account for the year ended 31 May 20X2. Use a minus sign for deductions, or where there is a loss to be distributed.
You must enter zeros where appropriate in order to obtain full marks.**

Picklist: Interest on drawings – G, Interest on drawings – S, Share of residual profit or loss – G, Share of residual profit or loss – S, Drawings – G, Drawings – S, Sales commission – G, Sales commission – S.

Partnership appropriation account for the year ended 31 May 20X2

	£
Profit or loss for appropriation	
Residual profit or loss available for distribution	
Share of residual profit or loss:	
Total residual profit or loss distributed	

(b) Prepare the current accounts for each partner for the year ended 31 May 20X2. Show clearly the balances carried down. You MUST enter zeros where appropriate in order to obtain full marks. Do NOT use brackets, minus signs or dashes.

Picklist: Balance b/d, Interest on drawings, Sales commission, Share of profit or loss, Drawings, Balance c/d.

Current accounts

Details	Gary £	Safina £	Details	Gary £	Safina £
▼			▼		
▼			▼		
▼			▼		
▼			▼		
▼			▼		
Total			Total		

Activity 6.4

This task is about final accounts for partnerships.

You are preparing the statement of financial position for DE Traders for the year ended 30 June 20X3.

The partners are Dan and Ed who share profits or losses in the ratio of 3:1. This is the only partnership agreement.

You have the final trial balance below. All of the necessary year-end adjustments have been made, except for the transfer of £10,520 net profit to the current accounts of each partner for the year ended.

Trial balance as at 30 June 20X3

	DR £	CR £
Fixtures and fittings - at cost	18,000	
Depreciation charges	4,500	
Accumulated depreciation - fixtures and fittings		9,000
Allowance for doubtful debts		310
Opening inventory	12,300	
Bank overdraft		1,450
Trade receivables	15,600	
Sales		58,900
Sales returns	800	
Irrecoverable debts	400	
Allowance for doubtful debts - adjustment	60	
VAT owed to HMRC		4,320
Trade payables		7,830
Carriage outwards	790	
Carriage inwards	540	
Purchase returns		250
Closing inventory	11,100	11,100
Purchases	18,900	
Current - D	1,240	
Current - E		260
Capital - D		24,000
Capital - E		16,000
Drawings - D	15,000	
Drawings - E	12,000	
Bank interest and charges	340	
Premises expenses	9,000	
Telephone expenses	2,900	
Staff wages	9,200	
Prepayments	750	
TOTAL	**133,420**	**133,420**

Prepare the statement of financial position for the partnership as at 30 June 20X3. Trade receivables are shown net of any allowance for doubtful debts. ONLY use minus signs for an overdrawn current account. Only whole pounds (£) must be entered do NOT use decimals.

Picklist: Fixtures and fittings, Closing inventory, Trade receivables, Prepayments, Capital accounts, Current accounts, Drawings, Bank overdraft, Trade payables, VAT owed to HMRC.

Statement of financial position as at 30 June 20X3

	Cost £	Accumulated depreciation £	Carrying amount £
Non-current assets			
⇩			
Current assets			
⇩			
⇩			
⇩			
⇩			
⇩			
Current liabilities			
⇩			
⇩			
⇩			
⇩			
⇩			
⇩			
Net current assets			
Net assets			
Financed by	Dan	Ed	Total
⇩			
⇩			

End of Task

7 Accounting for Partnership Goodwill

7.1 Introduction

This chapter will explain goodwill in accounting terms and why goodwill will change partners' capital account balances, when there is admission or retirement of a partner.

Exam tasks may expect you to calculate goodwill adjustments for admission or retirement of a partner, to enter goodwill adjustments in the ledger accounts and balance off these accounts as necessary.

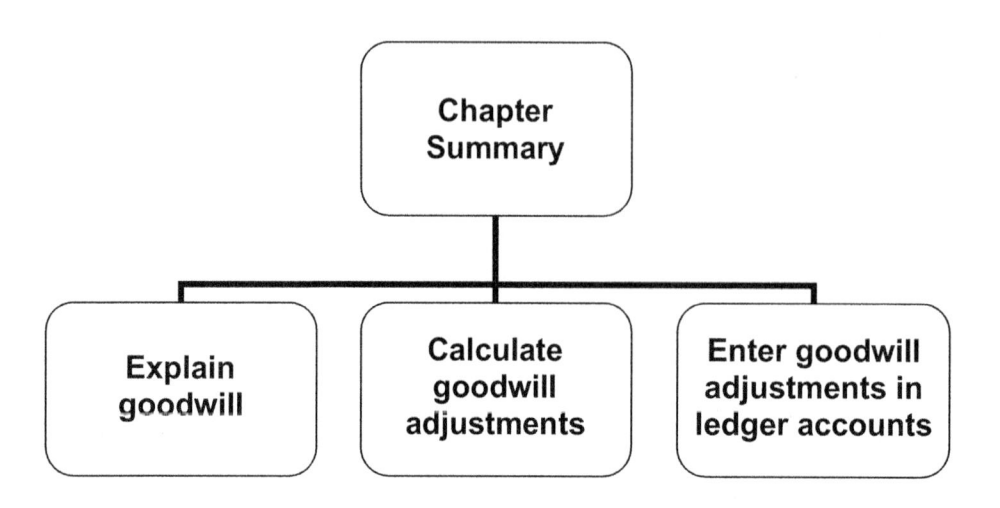

Chapter Summary
- Explain goodwill
- Calculate goodwill adjustments
- Enter goodwill adjustments in ledger accounts

7.2 Goodwill

If a sole trader business is sold, then its ownership will pass to a new buyer (owner), similarly a partner in a partnership can also sell their share of capital invested in a partnership. Goodwill is an asset accounted for when a business or share in a business is sold, it is the difference between the purchase price paid for the business less the net assets (capital) of the business. Goodwill represents a gain made on the sale of a business or the sale of a share in a business.

Reasons for goodwill to exist

- Excellent reputation of the business.
- Customer relationships and customer contacts built up over many years.
- Human assets e.g. skills, knowledge and creativity of employees.
- Ownership of technology or intellectual property.

The nature of goodwill

- Goodwill can be a highly valuable business asset.
- Goodwill is not an identifiable asset which is capable of being separated from the business.
- Goodwill is intangible, it has little or no physical substance and cannot be physically seen or touched.

Practice example

This example will calculate the value of goodwill for a partnership business. The following assets and liabilities exist for the partnership business. A buyer has offered £53,699 to purchase the entire business.

Assets and liabilities	£	
VAT owed from HMRC	3,401	Asset
Bank (not overdrawn)	5,078	Asset
Motor vehicle	19,000	Asset
Trade payables	3,000	Liability
Trade receivables	8,920	Asset
Inventory	10,800	Asset
Bank loan	10,500	Liability

Total assets	47,199
Total liabilities	13,500
Capital = Assets - Liabilities	33,699

The value of goodwill is the purchase price of £53,699 less net assets (capital) of business £33,699 = Goodwill of £20,000. The value of goodwill is not required to be calculated for exam tasks and the amount will always be provided in the task information.

7.3 Admission or retirement of a partner

Exam tasks may expect you to calculate goodwill adjustments for admission or retirement of a partner. In such cases the partnership business is not being sold, however, there may be inherent goodwill present in the partnership business which is not being evidenced because no purchase has been made. Goodwill in these situations must be accounted for even though there is no sale of the business.

A retiring partner will not want to leave with just their share of net assets (capital) in the partnership business, they will also want their share of goodwill that they have helped to build for the partnership business, perhaps over many years.

A new partner could also be admitted, in which case existing partners will want to be fairly compensated for the profit or loss share they are going to give up. Compensation for existing partners will need to ensure their share of goodwill that they have helped build in the business is recognised and accounted for.

Goodwill is a gain made on the business and the profit or loss sharing agreement between partners is used to work out each partners' share of the goodwill. Exam tasks will expect that goodwill is introduced into the accounting records of the partnership and then immediately eliminated.

Examples when goodwill is adjusted for in a partnership

- A change in the profit or loss sharing agreement between existing partners.
- Admission of a new partner.
- Retirement of an existing partner.
- Death of an existing partner.

How goodwill is introduced into the accounting records:

- **Debit** Goodwill account (increase asset) using the share of profit or loss for each partner in the old partnership.
- **Credit** Capital account (increase capital) using the share of profit or loss for each partner in the old partnership.

The share of goodwill for each partner is calculated using the old profit or loss sharing agreement in the old partnership.

How goodwill is eliminated from the accounting records:

- **Debit** Capital account (decrease capital) using the share of profit or loss for each partner in the new partnership.
- **Credit** Goodwill account (decrease asset) using the share of profit or loss for each partner in the new partnership.

The share of goodwill for each partner is calculated using the new profit or loss sharing agreement in the new partnership.

Practice example

You have the following information about a partnership business.

- Anne and Burt have been its owners for many years, trading as AB Partners.
- Anne and Burt currently share profits or losses equally.
- Charles was admitted on 31 March 20X2 as a new partner and invested £30,000 capital into the partnership business.
- Goodwill was valued at £50,000 and has not yet been entered in the accounting records.

The new partnership agreement will share profits or losses as follows:

Anne   50% share
Burt   30% share
Charles   20% share

The opening capital balances for Anne and Burt on 1 April 20X1 are included in the ledger accounts below. Goodwill is to be introduced into the accounting records on 31 March 20X2 and immediately eliminated.

Capital accounts

Details	Anne £	Burt £	Charles £	Details	Anne £	Burt £	Charles £
Goodwill				Balance b/d	15,000	10,000	
Balance c/d				Bank			
				Goodwill			
Total				Total			

Solution to practice example

Charles invested £30,000 capital into the partnership business. The double entry would be to debit the bank (increase asset) with £30,000 and to credit the capital account (increase capital) of Charles with £30,000. This entry has been made in the capital account of Charles below.

Capital accounts

Details	Anne £	Burt £	Charles £	Details	Anne £	Burt £	Charles £
				Balance b/d	15,000	10,000	
				Bank			30,000
Total				Total			

Goodwill introduced into the accounting records

Goodwill was valued at £50,000 and has not been entered in the accounting records. Goodwill is allocated to each partner using the old profit or loss share agreement from the old partnership. The old partnership was Anne and Burt who currently share profits or losses equally, so would each receive 50% share of the goodwill.

- Anne   50% share x £50,000 = £25,000 share of goodwill.
- Burt   50% share x £50,000 = £25,000 share of goodwill.

The double entry would be to debit goodwill (increase asset) and to credit the capital account (increase capital) of each partner with their share of goodwill. These entries have been made in the goodwill account and capital accounts of Anne and Burt shown below.

Goodwill

Details	£	Details	£
Capital - Anne	25,000		
Capital - Burt	25,000		
Total		Total	

Capital accounts

Details	Anne £	Burt £	Charles £	Details	Anne £	Burt £	Charles £
				Balance b/d	15,000	10,000	
				Bank			30,000
				Goodwill	25,000	25,000	
Total				Total			

Goodwill eliminated from the accounting records

Goodwill is eliminated by allocating to each partner a share of goodwill using the new profit or loss share agreement for the new partnership. The new partnership is Anne, Burt and Charles who share profits or losses 50%, 30% and 20% respectively.

- Anne   50% share x £50,000 = £25,000 share of goodwill.
- Burt   30% share x £50,000 = £15,000 share of goodwill.
- Charles   20% share x £50,000 = £10,000 share of goodwill.

The double entry would be to debit the capital account (decrease capital) of each partner with their share of goodwill and credit goodwill (decrease asset) to close down the goodwill account (eliminated). These entries have been made in the goodwill account and capital accounts of Anne, Burt and Charles shown below.

Goodwill

Details	£	Details	£
Capital - Anne	25,000	Capital - Anne	25,000
Capital - Burt	25,000	Capital - Burt	15,000
		Capital - Charles	10,000
Total	50,000	Total	50,000

Capital accounts

Details	Anne £	Burt £	Charles £	Details	Anne £	Burt £	Charles £
Goodwill	25,000	15,000	10,000	Balance b/d	15,000	10,000	
				Bank			30,000
				Goodwill	25,000	25,000	
Total				Total			

One way to remember goodwill adjustments for the goodwill account is... 'in with the old' (Debit Goodwill using the old profit share agreement) and 'out with the new' (Credit Goodwill using the new profit share agreement). The other side of the double entry will always be to the capital accounts of the partners. The accounting approach is the same regardless of whether there is admission or retirement of a partner.

The goodwill account illustrated above is now closed (eliminated) and the partners' capital accounts shown below are totalled and balanced.

Capital accounts

Details	Anne £	Burt £	Charles £	Details	Anne £	Burt £	Charles £
Goodwill	25,000	15,000	10,000	Balance b/d	15,000	10,000	
Balance c/d	15,000	20,000	20,000	Bank			30,000
				Goodwill	25,000	25,000	
Total	40,000	35,000	30,000	Total	40,000	35,000	30,000

- Anne had a 50% share of profit or losses in both the old and the new partnership agreement, since she has gained and lost nothing for her share of profits or losses, the balance of her capital account is unchanged.
- Burt had a 50% share in the old partnership agreement and a 30% share in the new partnership agreement, since he has lost some of his share of profits or losses, the balance of his capital account has increased to compensate.
- Charles had no share in the old partnership agreement and gained a 20% share in the new partnership agreement, since he has gained his share of profits or losses, the balance of his capital account has decreased to compensate any partners who have lost out, which was Burt.

Whether there is admission or retirement of a partner the process of accounting for goodwill is the same. Those partners who lose any share of profits or losses under the new agreement will be compensated and their capital account balances will increase. Those partners who gain any share of profits or losses under the new agreement will have their capital account balances decreased, because they will compensate other partners who lose out.

7.4 Accounting for retirement of a partner

If a partner has retired their capital and current account is no longer represented in the 'financed by' section of the statement of financial position because they are no longer a partner (owner).

Retirement is normally dealt with using the following process:

1. Goodwill adjustments are made to the capital accounts of each partner.
2. The capital account of the retiring partner is closed, and any balance is transferred to their current account (Debit Capital account and Credit Current account).
3. The current account of the retiring partner is closed, and any balance either paid off by the business (Debit Current account and Credit Bank), or transferred to a loan (liability) account (Debit Current account and Credit Loan).

Chapter activities

Activity 7.1

You have the following information about a partnership business.

Gary, Tufal and Safina have been its owners for many years, trading as GTS Partners.

Gary, Tufal and Safina currently share profits or losses using the following percentages:

- Gary   50%
- Tufal   30%
- Safina   20%

On the 31 January 20X2, Gary retired from the partnership. Goodwill was valued at £50,000 and has not yet been entered in the accounting records. Goodwill is to be introduced into the accounting records on 31 January 20X2 with the partnership change and then immediately eliminated.

When Gary retires, both Tufal and Safina will share profits or losses equally.

Prepare the goodwill account and capital accounts of each partner for the year ended 31 January 20X2, show clearly the individual entries for the introduction and elimination of goodwill. You must enter zeros where appropriate in order to obtain full marks.

Picklist: Balance b/d, Balance c/d, Bank, Capital - Gary, Capital - Tufal, Capital - Safina, Drawings, Current - Gary, Current - Tufal, Current - Safina, Goodwill.

Goodwill

Details	£	Details	£
Total		Total	

Capital accounts

Details	Gary £	Tufal £	Safina £	Details	Gary £	Tufal £	Safina £
				Balance b/d	35,000	25,000	20,000
Total				Total			

Activity 7.2

You have the following information about a partnership business.

Edward, Fred and Gerald have been its owners for many years, trading as EFG Partners.

Edward, Fred and Gerald currently share profits or losses in the ratio of 3:2:1 respectively.

On the 30 June 20X1, Gerald retired from the partnership. Goodwill was valued at £30,000 and has not yet been entered in the accounting records. Goodwill is to be introduced into the accounting records on 30 June 20X1 with the partnership change and then immediately eliminated.

When Gerald retires, both Edward and Fred will share profits or losses in the ratio of 2:1 respectively.

(a) Prepare the goodwill account for the year ended 30 June 20X1, showing clearly the individual entries for the introduction and elimination of goodwill.

Picklist: Balance b/d, Balance c/d, Bank, Capital - Edward, Capital - Fred, Capital - Gerald, Drawings, Current - Edward, Current - Fred, Current - Gerald, Goodwill.

Goodwill

Details	£	Details	£
Total		Total	

The capital account balances of each partner on 30 June 20X1 before adjusting for goodwill was as follows:

	£
Edward	40,000
Fred	20,000
Gerald	20,000

(b) Complete the following sentence about Fred's capital account after goodwill has been introduced and eliminated in the accounting records:

Fred's capital account balance as at 30 June 20X1 would be a [▼] of

£ [   ]

Picklist: Debit, Credit.

(c) Complete the following sentence about Gerald's capital account after goodwill has been introduced and eliminated in the accounting records:

Gerald capital account balance as at 30 June 20X1 would be a [▼] of

[   ] £

Picklist: Debit, Credit.

End of Task

8 Preparing Accounts for a Limited Company

8.1 Introduction

This chapter will explain the key differences between preparing accounts for a limited company and a sole trader. This chapter will explain the accounting standards that provide guidance to companies for the presentation of their financial statements and for their inventories and property, plant and equipment. Exam tasks will not require you to prepare final accounts for a company.

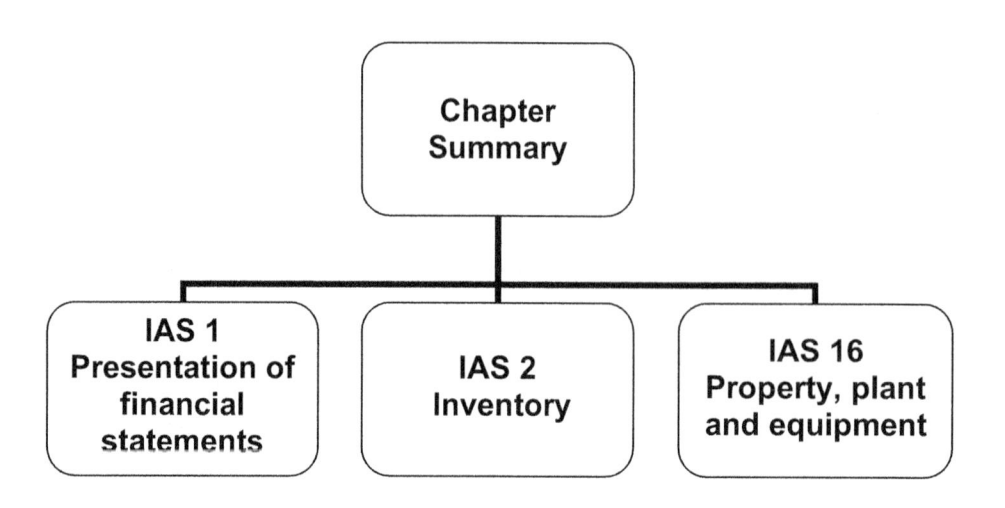

```
                    ┌──────────────┐
                    │   Chapter    │
                    │   Summary    │
                    └──────┬───────┘
          ┌────────────────┼────────────────┐
   ┌──────┴──────┐   ┌─────┴─────┐   ┌──────┴───────┐
   │    IAS 1    │   │   IAS 2   │   │    IAS 16    │
   │Presentation │   │ Inventory │   │Property,plant│
   │ of financial│   │           │   │and equipment │
   │ statements  │   │           │   │              │
   └─────────────┘   └───────────┘   └──────────────┘
```

8.2 The limited company

A company is a business that is run by a board of directors and owned by its shareholders. A company is a separate legal person that can enter into contracts, be sued or made bankrupt just like a real person.

Characteristics of a company

- A board of directors is appointed by the company shareholders to manage and control the company.
- Shareholders own shares (equity) in the company, which represents the ownership and voting rights of each shareholder.
- The company is a separate legal entity from its shareholders (owners).
- The company pays corporation tax on its profits earned.
- The company distributes profits earned by paying dividends to its shareholders.
- The representation of net assets (total assets - total liabilities) in the statement of financial position is called equity, which represents the capital invested by shareholders of the company.

Types of company

- A private limited company uses the standard abbreviation of 'Ltd' which stands for 'limited'. This type of company is private and cannot offer it shares for sale to the general public, shares can only be sold to existing shareholders and to private investors.
- A public limited company uses the standard abbreviation of 'Plc' which stands for 'public limited company'. This type of company offers its shares for sale to the general public. Its share price is publicly quoted on a registered exchange market such as the London stock exchange, where anyone can buy or sell the shares.

A company gives limited liability protection to its shareholders. Shareholders are legally responsible for the debts of a company, only to the extent of the amount they have invested personally for their shares. A shareholder (owner) can only lose what they have invested to buy their shares in the company, the personal assets of a shareholder are not at risk if the company fails.

Regulations applying to a limited company

A company is a separate legal person and must pay corporation tax on its profits earned, it must file an annual company tax return to HMRC.

Companies are regulated extensively by the Companies Act and Accounting Standards such as International Accounting Standards (IAS).

The Companies Act is the primary source of company law that governs companies in the UK. For example, it regulates the incorporation (formation) of a company and the directors' duties and responsibilities.

As a legal requirement a limited company needs to prepare financial statements at least annually and file them publicly at Companies House. Accounting standards regulate and govern extensively how company financial statements are prepared and presented. The main objective of accounting standards is to standardise accounting policies and principles that all companies must follow when preparing financial statements.

Objectives of accounting standards

- Ensure financial statements for all companies are comparable.
- Ensure all companies follow the same standardised rules.
- Ensure financial statements are credible, accurate, reliable and consistent.

8.3 IAS 1 Presentation of financial statements

IAS 1 sets out the overall requirements for the presentation of financial statements for companies, it gives guidelines for the structure and minimum requirements for the content of financial statements. IAS 1 requires a company to present a complete set of financial statements at least annually (including comparative amounts for the preceding year) and the main objective of this standard is to ensure the comparability of company financial statements.

The financial statements provide information about the financial position, financial performance and cash flows of the company, which is useful for users to make economic decisions.

Example of the content of financial statements

- Statement of profit or loss.
- Statement of financial position.
- Statement of changes in equity.
- Statement of cash flows.
- Supporting notes to the financial statements.
- Directors' report to the shareholders.
- Auditor's report (smaller companies may be exempt).

Supporting notes to the financial statements would comprise a summary of significant accounting policies and other explanatory information about the main figures which make up the financial statements. For example, only the carrying value for non-current assets appears in the statement of financial position of a company, but a much more detailed note would exist in the financial statements that will support this figure.

Notes are provided as part of the financial statements of a company to allow users to understand a clearer picture about the company's financial performance, position and cash-flows.

Exam tasks will not require the preparation of final accounts for a company but will expect you to understand the key differences between preparing accounts for a limited company and a sole trader.

Example of company financial statements

Statement of financial position as at 31 March 20X9

	20X9 £000	20X8 £000
Assets		
Non-current assets		
Property, plant and equipment	12,920	10,800
Current assets		
Inventories	738	340
Trade receivables	255	430
Cash and cash equivalents	273	670
Total assets	14,186	12,240
EQUITY AND LIABILITIES		
Equity		
Share capital (£1 ordinary shares)	6,000	5,000
Share premium account	3,000	2,000
Revaluation reserve	2,000	1,000
Retained earnings	2,403	2,189
Total equity	13,403	10,189
Non-current liabilities	500	1,500
Current liabilities		
Trade payables	192	403
Tax	161	148
Total liabilities	853	2,051
Total equity and liabilities	14,256	12,240

Statement of profit or loss for the year ended 31 March 20X9

	20X9 £000	20X8 £000
Revenue	2,450	2,310
Cost of sales	-845	-798
Gross profit	1,605	1,512
Distribution costs	-420	-433
Administrative expenses	-230	-221
Profit from operations	955	858
Finance costs	-80	-120
Profit before tax	875	738
Tax	-161	-148
Profit for the year	714	590

Final accounts for a sole trader are not governed by laws and accounting regulations. There is no definitive presentation for final accounts, or any specific accounting legislation that governs how sole trader final accounts should be prepared. In most cases, just a profit or loss account is prepared as basic information necessary for tax return purposes.

Key differences for limited company and sole trader accounts

- Financial statements for a limited company need to follow statutory formats with prescribed headings and terminology. There are no regulations that govern how sole trader accounts must be presented or what their minimum content must include.
- Company expenses must be classified according to rules and presented as either cost of sales, distribution costs or administration expenses in the statement of profit or loss. Sole traders can classify their expenses however they choose.
- A company is a separate legal person and will pay corporation tax on its profits earned, this is shown as a tax expense in the statement of profit or loss for a company. Sole traders pay income tax on profits earned by their own business and are responsible for submitting their own annual income tax returns to HMRC, there would be no tax shown in the statement of profit or loss for a sole trader.
- Only the carrying value of non-current assets appears in the statement of financial position for a company. Sole trader accounts normally show the original cost, accumulated depreciation and the carrying value of non-current assets in the statement of financial position.
- The financed by section for a company would show shareholders equity which represents the ownership (equity) of the company in the statement of financial position. The financed by section for a sole trader would show their capital account in the statement of financial position.
- Financial statements for a company need to be filed with Companies House where they are available for public inspection. A sole traders financial statements are their own private matter.

8.4 IAS 2 Inventory

IAS 2 regulates the accounting treatment and requirements for most types of inventory. Inventory is the cost of 'unsold goods for resale' (purchases) at the end of the accounting year. IAS 2 defines inventories as assets which are held for sale in the ordinary course of business.

IAS 2 outlines acceptable methods for determining the cost of inventory, such as the first-in first-out (FIFO) method and weighted average cost (AVCO) method. IAS 2 prohibits the use of the last-in last-out (LIFO) method due to potential distortions it has on a company's profitability and financial position.

IAS 2 states that inventory must be valued at 'the lower of its purchase cost or its 'net realisable value'. Net realisable value (NRV) means the estimated selling price of the inventory less any costs to complete its sale. Net realisable value is driven by the prudence concept. It is conservative that if any items of inventory cannot be sold for an amount more than its purchase cost, then the valuation of inventory is reduced to its net realisable value. Inventory value can be worth less than its purchase cost due to obsolescence, damage or falling market prices.

8.5 IAS 16 Property, plant and equipment

IAS 16 regulates the accounting treatment for most types of property, plant and equipment.

Examples of property, plant and equipment

- Buildings.
- Plant and equipment.
- Computer equipment.
- Office equipment.
- Furniture, fixtures and fittings.
- Motor vehicles.

IAS 16 defines tangible non-current assets as 'assets with physical substance and held for a continual (long-term) purpose'. Expenditure on non-current assets is capital expenditure, which means expenditure that is treated as an asset, not an expense in the accounting records of a business. Property, plant and equipment is initially measured at cost and should be depreciated over its useful life.

Chapter activities

Activity 8.1

Drag and drop to match the correct international accounting standard (IAS) to each explanation shown below.

Explanation	International Accounting Standard
Financial statements for a limited company need to follow statutory formats with prescribed headings and terminology.	
Non-current assets are initially measured at cost and should be depreciated over their useful life.	
Outlines acceptable methods for determining the cost of inventory.	

IAS 16

IAS 1

IAS 2

Activity 8.2

Show whether the following statements are true or false.

	TRUE	FALSE
IAS 2 states that inventory must be valued at 'the higher of its purchase cost or its 'net realisable value'.	☐	☐
The original cost, accumulated depreciation and the carrying value of non-current assets is shown on the statement of financial position for a company.	☐	☐
IAS 1 gives guidelines for the structure and minimum requirements for the content of company financial statements.	☐	☐

Activity 8.3

	TRUE	FALSE
A private limited company offers its shares for sale to the general public.	☐	☐
The representation of net assets for a company in the statement of financial position is called equity.	☐	☐
The Companies Act is the primary source of company law that governs companies in the UK.	☐	☐

End of Task

Solutions to Chapter Activities

Solutions to chapter 1 activities

Activity 1.1 - Solution

Charity	LLP
Board of Trustees	Members

Activity 1.2 - Solution

	TRUE	FALSE
The net assets of a charity are represented as the surplus of the charity in the statement of financial position.	☐	✓
A limited liability partnership gives unlimited liability for its members.	☐	✓
Partners can provide more investment, skills and expertise to make a partnership business more successful.	✓	☐

- The net assets of a charity are represented as the funds (not surplus) of the charity in the statement of financial position.
- A limited liability partnership gives limited (not unlimited) liability for its members.

Activity 1.3 - Solution

Advantage	Type of organisation
Tax exempt and does not pay tax on any surplus earned.	Charity
Full control and makes all the key business decisions.	Sole trader
Gives limited liability to its members.	LLP

Activity 1.4 - Solution

	TRUE	FALSE
The presentation of final accounts for a sole trader is governed by complex laws and accounting regulations.	☐	✓
There generally exists a statutory maximum of 20 partners allowed in a partnership.	✓	☐
A company is a separate legal person from the shareholders (owners) of the company.	✓	☐

The presentation of final accounts for a sole trader is **not** governed by complex laws and accounting regulations.

Activity 1.5 - Solution

	TRUE	FALSE
Profits earned from a partnership are distributed by each partner taking drawings from the business.	✓	
The net assets in the statement of financial position for a company can be represented as equity.	✓	
Charities are not regulated to the same extent as a company.		✓

Charities **are** regulated to the same extent as a company.

Solutions to chapter 2 activities

Activity 2.1 - Solution

Decline to discuss this matter with the close family friend.	✓
Advise the family friend of the possible takeover.	☐
Advise the family friend to hold on to their shares but don't advise them of the reasons.	☐

Activity 2.2 - Solution

Confidentiality	✓
Objectivity	☐
Integrity	☐

Activity 2.3 - Solution

To accept the task assigned because the client is a close friend.	☐
To accept the task assigned but make it known to the friend that the student does not possess the necessary experience to carry out the task assigned.	☐
To reject the task assigned but help the friend obtain competitive quotes from a qualified accountancy practice to carry out the work.	✓

Activity 2.4 - Solution

Obey the managers instruction without question.	☐
Present the errors that have been spotted and request a deadline extension.	☑
Resign from her position.	☐

Activity 2.5 - Solution

Do not inform the client and keep the inventory amount the same to make the accounts look good for the client.	☐
Tell the client but keep the inventory amount the same and make the accounts look good for the client.	☐
Tell the client and advise of the adjustment required and impact on profits.	☑

Activity 2.6 - Solution

	TRUE	FALSE
A customer may use the final accounts of a business it buys goods from, to assess the debts of the business and its ability to meet future loan repayments and interest.	☐	☑
Relevance and faithful representation are the fundamental qualitative characteristics of useful financial information.	☑	☐
The prudence concept is an accounting principle that exercises caution to avoid under estimating liabilities and expenses.	☑	☐

The first statement is a reason for a bank to use final accounts not a customer. A customer is more likely to assess any going concern problems of the business and its ability to continue to supply goods or services in the future.

Activity 2.7 - Solution

Explanation	Accounting principle
A business can continue to operate and remain in business for the foreseeable future, without significant threat of liquidation or closure.	Going concern
The transactions of a business and personal transactions of its owners, must be recorded separately for accounting purposes.	Separate entity
Final accounts recognise all sales income earned and all related expenses consumed for the same accounting year.	Accruals

Activity 2.8 - Solution

Explanation	Qualitative characteristic
Enables users to identify similarities and differences in business performance.	Comparability
Gives assurance to the user that the information provided is faithfully represented.	Verifiability
Ensures that information provided is capable of influencing and making a difference to the decisions of users.	Relevance

Activity 2.9 - Solution

Explanation	User
To assess the ability of the business to continue to supply goods or services in the future.	Customer
To assess how much profit has been generated by the business and the value of its net assets.	Shareholder
To assess the ability of the business to meet future loan repayments and interest.	Bank

Activity 2.10 - Solution

	TRUE	FALSE
Investors, lenders and trade suppliers would be the primary users of final accounts.	✓	☐
The enhancing qualitative characteristics of useful financial information include comparability, verifiability and faithful representation.	☐	✓
The accruals concept is an accounting principle that dictates that if a transaction has a significant impact on the final accounts, then it should be recognised.	☐	✓

The four 'enhancing' qualitative characteristics include comparability, verifiability, timeliness and understandability (not faithful representation, this would be a 'fundamental' not enhancing characteristic). The materiality (not accruals) concept is an accounting principle that dictates that if a transaction has a significant impact on the final accounts, then it should be recognised.

Solutions to chapter 3 activities

Activity 3.1 - Solution

Record these transactions in the sales ledger control account and show the balance carried down.

Sales ledger control account

Details	Amount £	Details	Amount £
Balance b/d	6782	Bank	17822
Sales	24021	Sales returns	3410
		Discounts allowed	1244
		Balance c/d	8327
Total	30803	Total	30803

Activity 3.2 - Solution

Record these transactions in the purchases ledger control account and show the balance carried down.

Purchases ledger control account

Details	Amount £	Details	Amount £
Bank	8822	Balance b/d	7830
Purchases returns	450	Purchases	14521
Discounts received	559		
Balance c/d	12520		
Total	22351	Total	22351

Activity 3.3 - Solution

Complete the VAT control account by placing the entries on the debit or credit side:

- enter the VAT transactions for the month
- show the balance carried down and whether it will be a debit or credit balance
- insert the total that will be shown in both the debit and credit columns after the account has been balanced

VAT control account

Details	Amount £	Details	Amount £
Purchases daybook	1299	Balance b/d	2350
Sales returns day book	230	Sales daybook	3492
Bank	2884	Purchases returns daybook	56
Discounts allowed	455	Discounts received	325
Balance c/d	1355		
Total	6223	Total	6223

Activity 3.4 - Solution

(a) Using only the figures supplied, find the closing balance for the sales ledger control account for the year ended 30 June 20X8.

Sales ledger control account

	£		£
Balance b/d	8,500	Sales returns	900
Sales	67,200	Discounts allowed	2,880
		Purchase ledger control	500
		Bank	45,620
		Balance c/d	25,800
	75,700		75,700

(b) Find the cash purchases figure including VAT by preparing the bank account for the year ended 30 June 20X8.

Bank

	£		£
Balance b/d	3,402	Purchases ledger control	19,655
Sales ledger control	45,620	VAT	6,711
		Motor expenses	1,490
		Staff wages	3,025
		Loan repayment	1,500
		Drawings	3,500
		Bank charges and interest	430
		Cash purchases (missing figure)	5,400
		Balance c/d	7,311
	49,022		49,022

(c) Find the total discounts received figure including VAT by preparing the purchase ledger control account for the year ended 30 June 20X8.

Purchases ledger control account

	£		£
Purchases returns	3,600	Balance b/d	6,550
Bank	19,655	Purchases	39,264
Sales ledger control	500		
Discounts received (missing figure)	2,400		
Balance c/d	19,659		
	45,814		45,814

(d) Using only the figures from the task information provided, find the closing balance on the VAT account for the year ended 30 June 20X8. Note: the business is not charged VAT on loan repayments, wages or bank charges and interest.

VAT account

	£		£
Bank	6,711	Balance b/d	5,341
Motor expenses	248	Sales	11,200
Purchases	6,544	Purchase returns	600
Discounts allowed	480		
Sales returns	150		
Balance c/d	3,008		
	17,141		17,141

Only the VAT figures from the task information provided should be included in the VAT control account, therefore the VAT on the missing cash purchases figure (part b) and missing discounts received figure (part c) should be ignored in this task.

Activity 3.5 - Solution

(a) Find the total sales returns by preparing the sales ledger control account for the year ended 31 January 20X5.

Sales ledger control account

	£		£
Balance b/d	25760	Sales returns daybook	8758
Sales daybook	93864	Bank	66544
		Irrecoverable debts	3600
		Purchases ledger control	4000
		Balance c/d	36722
	119624		119624

The missing figure for sales returns is £8,758 and calculated by totalling and balancing the control account after all items including the balance b/d and c/d are entered in the control account.

(b) Find the total purchases by preparing the purchase ledger control account for the year ended 31 January 20X5.

Purchase ledger control account

	£		£
Purchase returns daybook	600	Balance b/d	9522
Bank	43200	Purchase daybook	56950
Sales ledger control	4000		
Balance c/d	18672		
	66472		66472

The missing figure for purchases is £56,950 and calculated by totalling and balancing the control account after all items including the balance b/d and c/d are entered in the control account.

(c) Assuming there are no year adjustments, what would be the opening bank account balance in the general ledger as at 1 February 20X5. Do NOT enter a negative figure.

Bank account balance 1 February 20X5 £8247.

Picklist: debit.

Workings

Bank

	£		£
Balance b/d	14,543	Payments	73,366
Receipts	67,070	Balance c/d	8,247
Totals	81,613	Totals	81,613
Balance b/d	8,247		

Solutions to chapter 4 activities

Activity 4.1 - Solution

(a) Calculate the cost of goods sold for the year ended 31 March 20X9.

£240,000.

Remove any VAT amounts from sales or purchases figures, if inclusive of VAT.

- Sales inclusive of VAT was £360,000 x 1/6 = VAT £60,000. Sales exclusive of VAT is £300,000 (£360,000 - £60,000).
- Purchases inclusive of VAT was £252,000 x 1/6 = VAT £42,000. Purchases exclusive of VAT is £210,000 (£252,000 - £42,000).

Construct a trading account and include all information you have from the task.

	£	£
Sales (given)		300,000
Less: Cost of sales		
Opening inventory	48,000	
Purchases (given)	210,000	
(£28,000 + £70,000)	258,000	
Closing inventory (balancing figure, £258,000 - £240,000)	-18,000	
Cost of goods sold (£300,000 - £60,000)		240,000
Gross profit (20% x £300,000)		60,000

Use sales margin to determine the gross profit and the cost of sales figure.

- 20% sales margin means that gross profit is 20% of sales.
- Sales £300,000 ÷ 100% x 20% = £60,000 gross profit.
- The cost of sales figure can now be calculated as a balancing figure. Cost of sales is £240,000 (Sales £300,000 - Gross profit £60,000).

(b) Calculate the value of the closing inventory destroyed in the fire.

£16,500.

If opening inventory and purchases added together is £258,000 and cost of sales is £240,000, the final figure for closing inventory must be £258,000 - £240,000 = £18,000.

- The value of closing inventory before the fire should be £18,000.
- The value of closing inventory after the fire was £1,500.
- The value of closing inventory destroyed in the fire was £16,500 (£18,000 - £1,500).

Activity 4.2 - Solution

(a) Calculate the value of purchases for the year ended 30 June 20X7.

£263,830.

- Inventory levels increased by £21,220.
- When inventory levels increase, closing inventory must be higher than opening inventory, £21,220 less is charged as cost of sales, compared to purchases.
- £21,220 is added to cost of sales to calculate the missing figure for purchases. Purchases would be £263,830 (£242,610 + £21,220).

Another logical way of dealing with the above problem would be to construct a working for cost of sales, like the one shown below. Insert the cost of sales figure of £242,610 and make up an assumption about the value of opening inventory. The workings show that opening inventory of £10,000 is selected as a 'made up' figure and so to force things to work, the closing inventory figure would be £31,220 because inventory levels increased by £21,220. Purchases can then be calculated as a balancing figure.

	£
Opening inventory (made up figure)	10,000
Purchases (final balancing figure, £273,830 - £10,000)	263,830
(£242,610 cost of sales + £31,220 closing inventory) =	273,830
Closing inventory (increase £10,000 opening inventory by £21,220)	-31,220
Cost of goods sold (given)	242,610

You can select any value of opening inventory in the approach used above, but do need to ensure that closing inventory is increased or decreased by the right amount, compared to opening inventory.

(b) Calculate the missing sales figure to go in the trial balance as at 30 June 20X7.

£339,654.

- Cost of goods sold for the year ended 30 June 20X7 was £242,610.
- Mark-up can be used to determine the gross profit figure. 40% mark-up means that gross profit is 40% of cost of sales. Cost of sales £242,610 ÷ 100% x 40% = £97,044 gross profit.
- Sales can be calculated by adding together the cost of sales £242,610 and the gross profit £97,044. Sales is £339,654 (£242,610 + £97,044).

Activity 4.3 - Solution

Calculate the original cost of the goods sold to the customer excluding VAT. Round your answer to the nearest 2 decimal places.

£937.50.

- The £1,500 sale price includes VAT so calculate the VAT amount and take this amount off the sale price. £1,500 x 1/6 = £250 VAT. Sales excluding VAT would be £1,500 - £250 = £1,250. If we can now find gross profit, we can derive the cost of the goods sold.
- Sales margin can be used to determine the gross profit figure. 25% margin means that gross profit is 25% of the sale price. Sale price £1,250 ÷ 100% x 25% = £312.50 gross profit earned from the goods sold.
- The cost of goods sold is calculated as the difference between the sale price £1,250 and the gross profit of £312.50. The cost of the goods sold is £937.50 (£1,250 - £312.50).

Activity 4.4 - Solution

Calculate sales for the year ended 31 January 20X2. Round your answer to the nearest whole pound.

£272,700.

- Inventory levels decreased by £21,500.
- When inventory levels decrease, closing inventory must be lower than opening inventory and £21,500 more is charged as cost of sales, compared to purchases.
- £21,500 is added to purchases to calculate the missing figure for cost of sales. Cost of sales would be £202,000 (£180,500 + £21,500).

Another logical way of dealing with the above problem would be to construct a working for a trading account, like the one shown below. Insert the purchases figure of £180,500 and make up an assumption about the value of opening inventory. The workings show that opening inventory of £30,000 is selected as a 'made up' figure and so to force things to work, the closing inventory figure would be £8,500 because inventory levels decreased by £21,500. Cost of sales can then be calculated as a balancing figure.

	£	£
Sales (final balance for missing figure, £70,700 + £202,000)		272,700
Less: Cost of sales		
Opening inventory (made up figure)	30,000	
Purchases (given)	180,500	
(£30,000 + £180,500)	210,500	
Closing inventory (decrease £30,000 opening inventory by £21,500)	-8,500	
Cost of goods sold (£210,500 - £8,500)		202,000
Gross profit (35% x £202,000)		70,700

You can select any value of opening inventory in the approach used above, but do need to ensure that closing inventory is increased or decreased by the right amount, compared to opening inventory.

- Cost of goods sold for the year ended 31 January 20X2 was £202,000 as per the workings above.
- Mark-up can be used to determine the gross profit figure. 35% mark-up means that gross profit is 35% of cost of sales. Cost of sales £202,000 ÷ 100% x 35% = £70,700 gross profit.
- Sales can be calculated by adding together the cost of sales £202,000 and the gross profit of £70,700. Sales is £272,700 (£202,000 + £70,700).

Solutions to chapter 5 activities

Activity 5.1 - Solution

Statement of financial position as at 30 June 20X3

	Cost £	Accumulated depreciation £	Carrying amount £
Non-current assets			
Fixtures and fittings	18,000	9,000	9,000
Current assets			
Closing inventory		11,100	
Trade receivables (£15,600 - £310)		15,290	
Prepayments		750	
		27,140	
Current liabilities			
Bank overdraft	1,450		
Trade payables	7,830		
VAT owed to HMRC	4,320		
		13,600	
Net current assets			13,540
Net assets			22,540
Financed by			
Opening capital			24,020
Profit for the year			10,520
Drawings			12,000
Closing capital			22,540

Statement of profit or loss for the year ended 30 June 20X3

	£	£
Sales revenue (£58,900 - £800)		58,100
Opening inventory	12,300	
Purchases (£18,900 + £540 - £250)	19,190	
Closing inventory	-11,100	
Cost of goods sold		20,390
Gross profit		37,710
Add:		
Less:		
Depreciation charges	4,500	
Irrecoverable debts	400	
Allowance for doubtful debts - adjustment	60	
Carriage outwards	790	
Bank interest and charges	340	
Premises expenses	9,000	
Telephone expenses	2,900	
Staff wages	9,200	
Total expenses		27,190
Net profit or loss		10,520

Activity 5.2 - Solution

Statement of financial position as at 31 August 20X8

	Cost £	Accumulated depreciation £	Carrying amount £
Non-current assets			
Motor vehicles	25,000	10,000	15,000
Current assets			
Closing inventory		5,500	
Trade receivables (£2,500 - £200)		2,300	
VAT owing from HMRC		1,240	
Bank		7,620	
		16,660	
Current liabilities			
Trade payables	5,490		
Accruals	2,000		
		7,490	
Net current assets			9,170
Net assets			24,170
Financed by			
Opening capital			50,300
Loss for the year			5,630
Drawings			20,500
Closing capital			24,170

Statement of profit or loss for the year ended 31 August 20X8

	£	£
Sales revenue (£34,200 - £2,800)		31,400
Opening inventory	5,000	
Purchases	19,500	
Closing inventory	-5,500	
Cost of goods sold		19,000
Gross profit		12,400
Add:		
Interest received	250	
		250
Less:		
Depreciation charges	5,000	
Irrecoverable debts	1,000	
Allowance for doubtful debts - adjustment	-120	
Advertising	5,000	
Telephone expenses	2,900	
Motor vehicle expenses	4,500	
Total expenses		18,280
Net profit or loss		-5,630

Activity 5.3 - Solution

Capital account

	£		£
Balance c/d	31,730	Bank	10,000
		Motor vehicles	7,500
		Profit or loss account	14,230
	31,730		31,730

Activity 5.4 - Solution

Indicate for each transaction below whether it would be a debit entry, or credit entry, or no posting made to the capital account of a sole trader, in the general ledger. Choose ONE answer for each transaction below.

	Debit	Credit	No posting
Drawings for the year ended	☑	☐	☐
A loss for the year ended	☑	☐	☐
Payment of business expenses through the business bank account	☐	☐	☑
A personal motor vehicle introduced by the owner	☐	☑	☐

Activity 5.5 - Solution

Use drag and drop to shown the correct double entry if business goods for resale are taken for personal use by the owner of the business.

| Purchases returns |

| Capital |

Debit
Drawings

Credit
Purchases

Activity 5.6 - Solution

Complete the capital account for the year ended 31 August 20X2. Show clearly the balance carried down to the next financial year.

Capital account

	£		£
Profit or loss account	12,510	Balance b/d	34,900
Drawings	16,000		
Balance c/d	6,390		
	34,900		34,900

Net assets means total assets - total liabilities and according to the accounting equation (Assets - Liabilities = Capital), if the net assets of the business on 1 September 20X1 was £34,900, then the balance b/d for the capital account must also be £34,900.

Solutions to chapter 6 activities

Activity 6.1 - Solution

(a) Prepare a partnership appropriation account for the year ended 31 August 20X6. Use a minus sign for deductions, or where there is a loss to be distributed. You must enter zeros where appropriate in order to obtain full marks.

	£
Profit or loss for appropriation	39,500
Interest on capital – C	-4,000
Interest on capital – D	-1,600
Salary – C	0
Salary – D	-15,000
Residual profit or loss available for distribution	18,900
Share of residual profit or loss:	
Share of residual profit or loss – C (£18,900 ÷ 3 x 2)	12,600
Share of residual profit loss – D (£18,900 ÷ 3 x 1)	6,300
Total residual profit or loss distributed	18,900

(b) Prepare the current accounts for each partner for the year ended 31 August 20X6. Show clearly the balances carried down. You MUST enter zeros where appropriate in order to obtain full marks. Do NOT use brackets, minus signs or dashes.

Details	Charlie £	David £	Details	Charlie £	David £
Balance b/d		2,350	Balance b/d	4,600	
Drawings	24,000	24,000	Interest on capital	4,000	1,600
			Salaries	0	15,000
			Share of profit or loss	12,600	6,300
			Balance c/d	2,800	3,450
Total	24,000	26,350	Total	24,000	26,350

Current accounts for each partner are overdrawn for the year ended 31 August 20X6.

Activity 6.2 - Solution

(a) Prepare a partnership appropriation account for the year ended 30 April 20X5. Use a minus sign for deductions, or where there is a loss to be distributed. You must enter zeros where appropriate in order to obtain full marks.

	£
Profit or loss for appropriation	-5,500
Interest on capital – B	-1,000
Interest on capital – V	-1,500
Salary – B (£1,000 per month x 12 months)	-12,000
Salary – V (£500 per month x 12 months)	-6,000
Residual profit or loss available for distribution	-26,000
Share of residual profit or loss:	
Share of residual profit or loss – C (£26,000 ÷ 2)	-13,000
Share of residual profit loss – D (£26,000 ÷ 2)	-13,000
Total residual profit or loss distributed	-26,000

(b) Prepare the current accounts for each partner for the year ended 30 April 20X5. Show clearly the balances carried down. You MUST enter zeros where appropriate in order to obtain full marks.

Current accounts

Details	Ben £	Vera £	Details	Ben £	Vera £
Balance b/d	1,450		Balance b/d		3,340
Drawings	18,000	12,000	Interest on capital	1,000	1,500
Share of profit or loss	13,000	13,000	Salaries	12,000	6,000
			Balance c/d	19,450	14,160
Total	32,450	25,000	Total	32,450	25,000

Current accounts for each partner are overdrawn for the year ended 30 April 20X5.

Activity 6.3 - Solution

(a) Prepare a partnership appropriation account for the year ended 31 May 20X2. Use a minus sign for deductions, or where there is a loss to be distributed. You must enter zeros where appropriate in order to obtain full marks.

	£
Profit or loss for appropriation	11,200
Interest on drawings – G	1,500
Interest on drawings – S	650
Sales commission – G	-12,000
Sales commission – S	-4,500
Residual profit or loss available for distribution	-3,150
Share of residual profit or loss:	
Share of residual profit or loss – G (£3,150 ÷ (3 + 2) x 3	-1,890
Share of residual profit or loss – S (£3,150 ÷ (3 + 2) x 2	-1,260
Total residual profit or loss distributed	-3,150

(b) Prepare the current accounts for each partner for the year ended 31 May 20X2. Show clearly the balances carried down. You MUST enter zeros where appropriate in order to obtain full marks. Do NOT use brackets, minus signs or dashes.

Current accounts

Details	Gary £	Safina £	Details	Gary £	Safina £
Interest on drawings	1,500	650	Balance b/d	3,550	6,310
Drawings	15,000	6,500	Sales commission	12,000	4,500
Share of profit or loss	1,890	1,260	Balance c/d	2,840	
Balance c/d		2,400			
Total	18,390	10,810	Total	18,390	10,810

The current account for Gary is overdrawn for the year ended 31 May 20X2.

Activity 6.4 - Solution

Statement of financial position as at 30 June 20X3

	Cost £	Accumulated depreciation £	Carrying amount £
Non-current assets			
Fixtures and fittings	18,000	9,000	9,000
Current assets			
Closing inventory		11,100	
Trade receivables (£15,600 - £310)		15,290	
Prepayments		750	
		27,140	
Current liabilities			
Bank overdraft	1,450		
Trade payables	7,830		
VAT owed to HMRC	4,320		
		13,600	
Net current assets			13,540
Net assets			22,540
Financed by	Dan	Ed	Total
Capital accounts	24,000	16,000	40,000
Current accounts	-8,350	-9,110	-17,460
	15,650	6,890	22,540

Share of profit or loss:

- Dan £10,520 net profit ÷ (3 + 1) x 3 = £7,890.
- Ed £10,520 net profit ÷ (3 + 1) x 1 = £2,630.

Current account workings:

Current accounts

Details	Dan £	Ed £	Details	Dan £	Ed £
Balance b/d	1,240		Balance b/d		260
Drawings	15,000	12,000	Share of profit or loss	7,890	2,630
			Balance c/d	8,350	9,110
Total	16,240	12,000	Total	16,240	12,000

Both current accounts are overdrawn for the year ended 30 June 20X3.

Solutions to chapter 7 activities

Activity 7.1 - Solution

Goodwill

Details	£	Details	£
Capital - Gary	25,000	Capital - Tufal	25,000
Capital - Tufal	15,000	Capital - Safina	25,000
Capital - Safina	10,000		
Total	50,000	Total	50,000

Goodwill introduced into the accounting records

Goodwill was valued at £50,000 and has not been entered in the accounting records. Goodwill will be allocated to each partner using the old profit or loss agreement from the old partnership. Gary, Tufal and Safina currently share profits or losses using the following percentages:

- Gary 50% share x £50,000 = £25,000 share of goodwill.
- Tufal 30% share x £50,000 = £15,000 share of goodwill.
- Safina 20% share x £50,000 = £10,000 share of goodwill.

The double entry would be to debit goodwill (increase asset) and to credit the capital account (increase capital) of each partner with their share of goodwill.

Goodwill eliminated from the accounting records

Goodwill will be eliminated by allocating to each partner a share of goodwill using the new profit or loss agreement for the new partnership. The new partnership is Tufal and Safina will share profits or losses equally.

- Tufal   50% share x £50,000 = £25,000 share of goodwill.
- Safina   50% share x £50,000 = £25,000 share of goodwill.

The double entry would be to debit the capital account (decrease capital) of each partner with their share of goodwill and credit goodwill (decrease asset) to close down the goodwill account (eliminated).

Capital accounts

Details	Gary £	Tufal £	Safina £	Details	Gary £	Tufal £	Safina £
Goodwill	0	25,000	25,000	Balance b/d	35,000	25,000	20,000
Balance c/d	60,000	15,000	5,000	Goodwill	25,000	15,000	10,000
Total	60,000	40,000	30,000	Total	60,000	40,000	30,000

Activity 7.2 - Solution

(a) Prepare the goodwill account for the year ended 30 June 20X1, showing clearly the individual entries for the introduction and elimination of goodwill.

Goodwill

Details	£	Details	£
Capital - Edward	15,000	Capital - Edward	20,000
Capital - Fred	10,000	Capital - Fred	10,000
Capital - Gerald	5,000		
Total	30,000	Total	30,000

Goodwill introduced into the accounting records

Goodwill was valued at £30,000 and has not been entered in the accounting records. Goodwill will be allocated to each partner using the old profit or loss agreement from the old partnership. Edward, Fred and Gerald share profits or losses in the ratio of 3:2:1 respectively (3 + 2 + 1 = 6).

- Edward   3 x (£30,000 ÷ 6) = £15,000 share of goodwill.
- Fred   2 x (£30,000 ÷ 6) = £10,000 share of goodwill.
- Gerald   1 x (£30,000 ÷ 6) = £5,000 share of goodwill.

The double entry would be to debit goodwill (increase asset) and to credit the capital account (increase capital) of each partner with their share of goodwill.

Goodwill eliminated from the accounting records

Goodwill will be eliminated by allocating to each partner a share of goodwill using the new profit or loss agreement for the new partnership. When Gerald retires, both Edward and Fred will share profits or losses in the ratio of 2:1 respectively (2 + 1 = 3).

- Edward   2 x (£30,000 ÷ 3) = £20,000 share of goodwill.
- Fred   1 x (£30,000 ÷ 3) = £10,000 share of goodwill.

The double entry would be to debit the capital account (decrease capital) of each partner with their share of goodwill and credit goodwill (decrease asset) to close down the goodwill account (eliminated).

Workings for capital accounts of each partner

Capital accounts

Details	Edward £	Fred £	Gerald £	Details	Edward £	Fred £	Gerald £
Goodwill	20,000	10,000	0	Balance b/d	40,000	20,000	20,000
Balance c/d	35,000	20,000	25,000	Goodwill	15,000	10,000	5,000
Total	55,000	30,000	25,000	Total	55,000	30,000	25,000

(b) Complete the following sentence about Fred's capital account after goodwill has been introduced and eliminated in the accounting records:

Fred's capital account balance as at 30 June 20X1 would be a Credit of £20,000.

(c) Complete the following sentence about Gerald's capital account after goodwill has been introduced and eliminated in the accounting records:

Gerald's capital account balance as at 30 June 20X1 would be a Credit of £25,000.

Solutions to chapter 8 activities

Activity 8.1 - Solution

Explanation	International Accounting Standard
Financial statements for a limited company need to follow statutory formats with prescribed headings and terminology.	IAS 1
Non-current assets are initially measured at cost and should be depreciated over their useful life.	IAS 16
Outlines acceptable methods for determining the cost of inventory.	IAS 2

Activity 8.2 - Solution

	TRUE	FALSE
IAS 2 states that inventory must be valued at 'the higher of its purchase cost or its 'net realisable value'.		✓
The original cost, accumulated depreciation and the carrying value of non-current assets is shown on the statement of financial position for a company.		✓
IAS 1 gives guidelines for the structure and minimum requirements for the content of company financial statements.	✓	

IAS 2 states that inventory must be valued at 'the lower (not higher) of its purchase cost or its 'net realisable value'. Only the carrying value of non-current assets is shown on the statement of financial position for a company.

Activity 8.3 - Solution

	TRUE	FALSE
A private limited company offers its shares for sale to the general public.	☐	✓
The representation of net assets for a company in the statement of financial position is called equity.	✓	☐
The Companies Act is the primary source of company law that governs companies in the UK.	✓	☐

A public (not private) limited company offers its shares for sale to the general public.

Printed in Great Britain
by Amazon